inkventiva

Women of the World
Color Diversity

Let your colors bring out the beauty and
uniqueness of these women.

This book belongs to

_____

_____

Welcome to Women of the World, Color Diversity

We want you to enjoy every coloring page to the fullest, so here are some tips and tricks to help you do just that. It's important to remember that to avoid bleeding, we recommend placing paper or cardboard behind the coloring drawing. That way, you can let your creativity run wild without worrying about smudging the page.
You can use any coloring tool available. The important thing is that you enjoy the process and experiment with different techniques and color combinations!

When you are done coloring, feel free to frame your favorite pages or use them to make cards or decorate walls. We're sure your work will be stunning!

So take your time, enjoy every moment of this coloring experience and let your creativity flow. We guarantee it will be an exciting and rewarding experience!

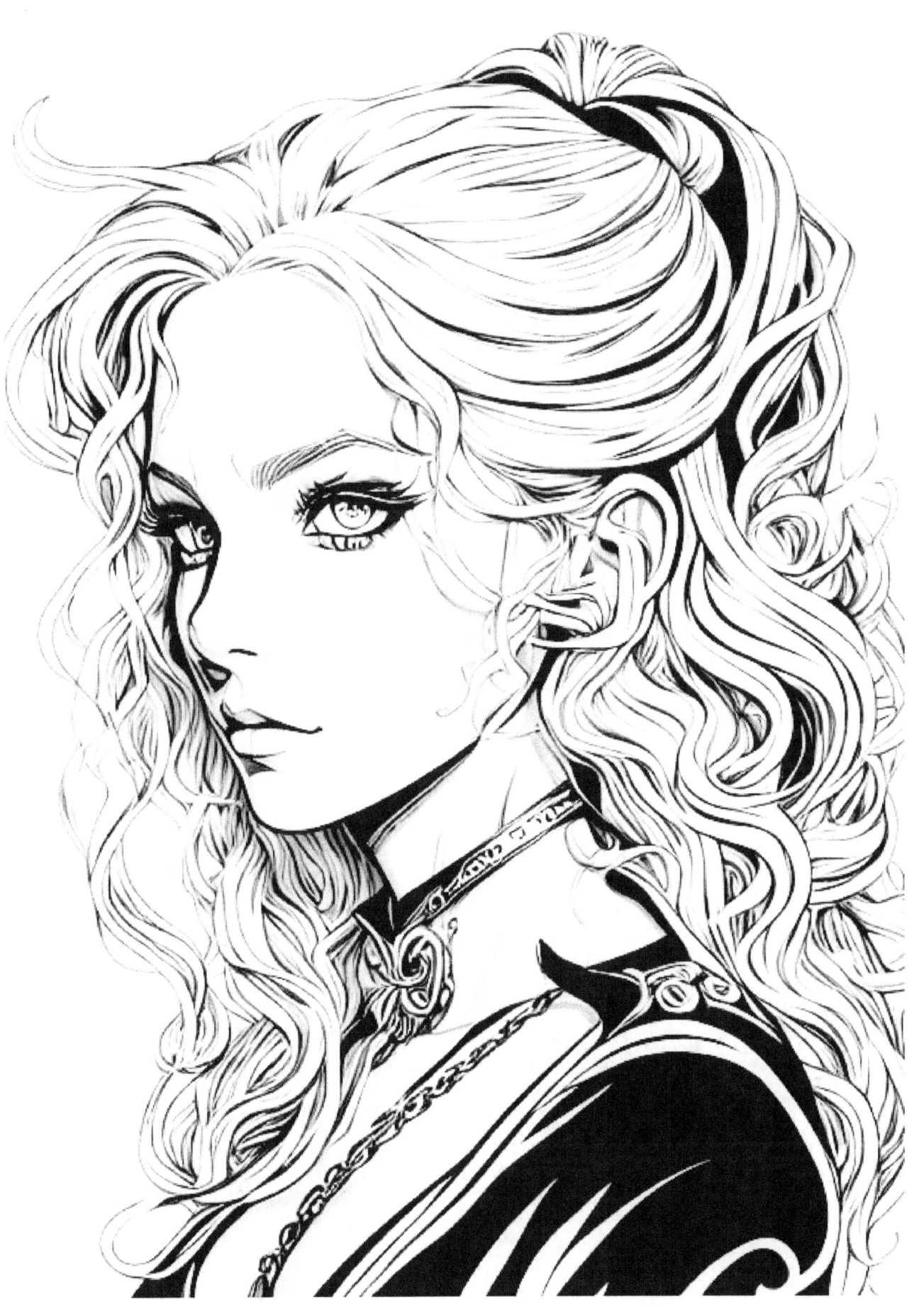

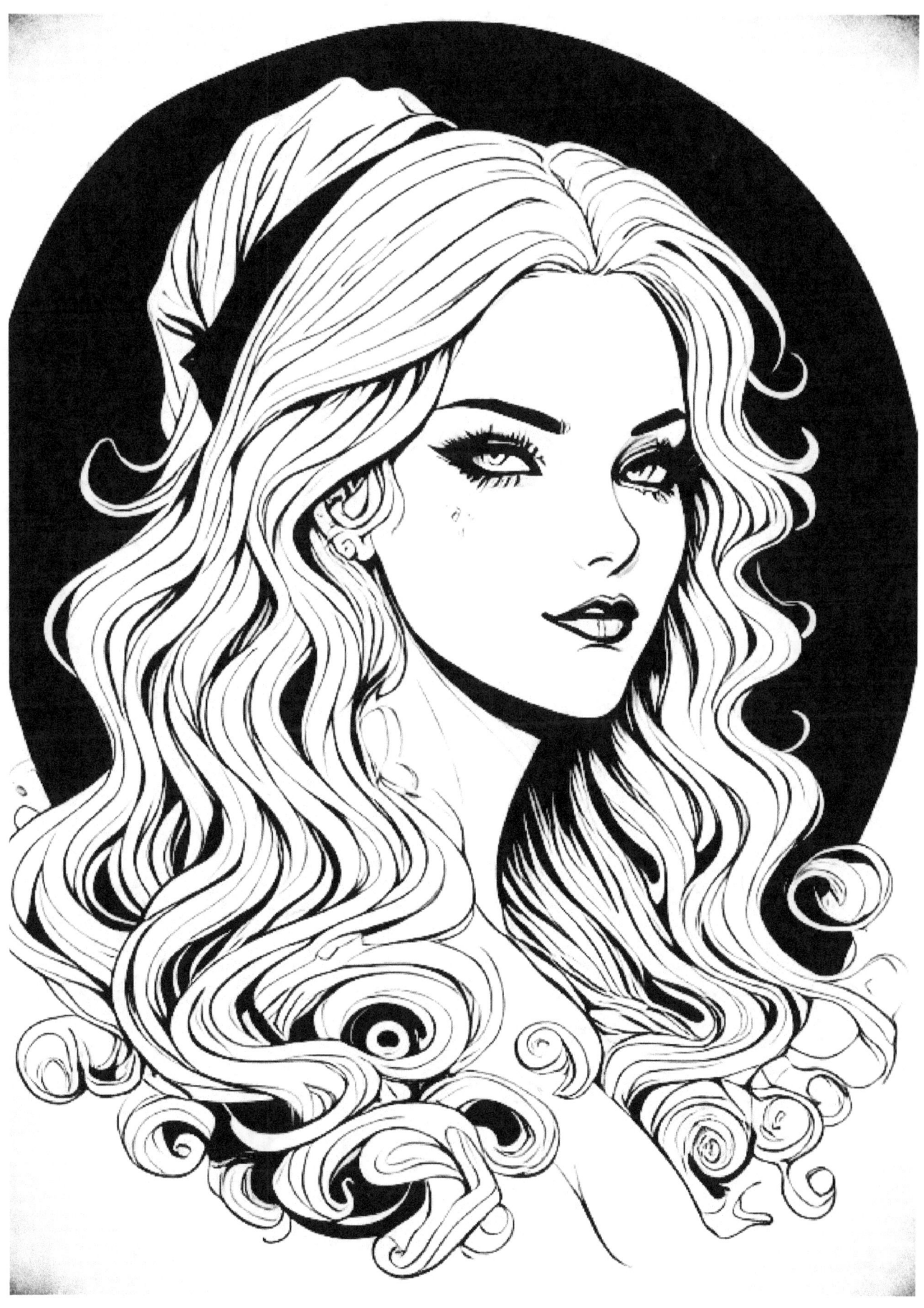

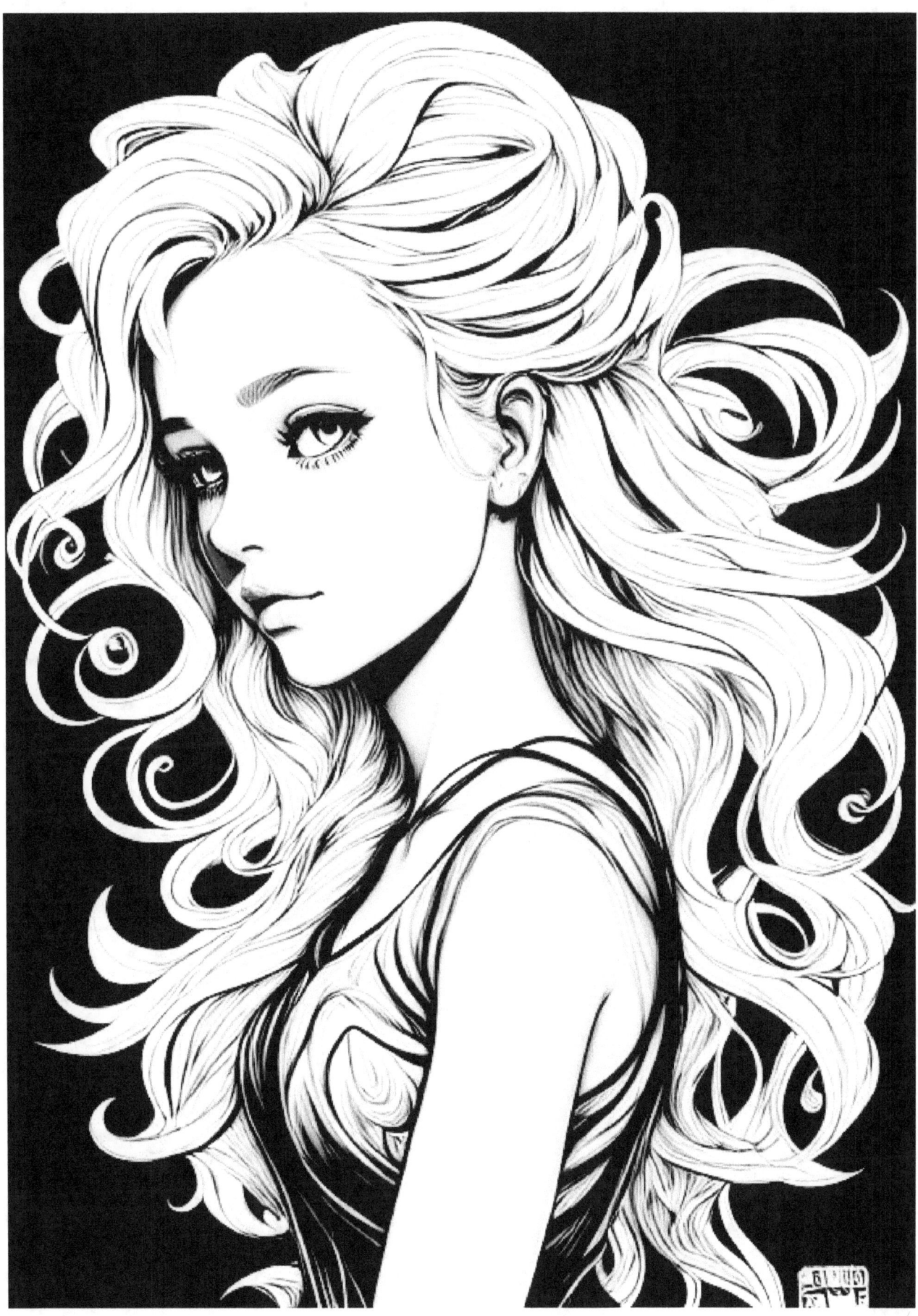

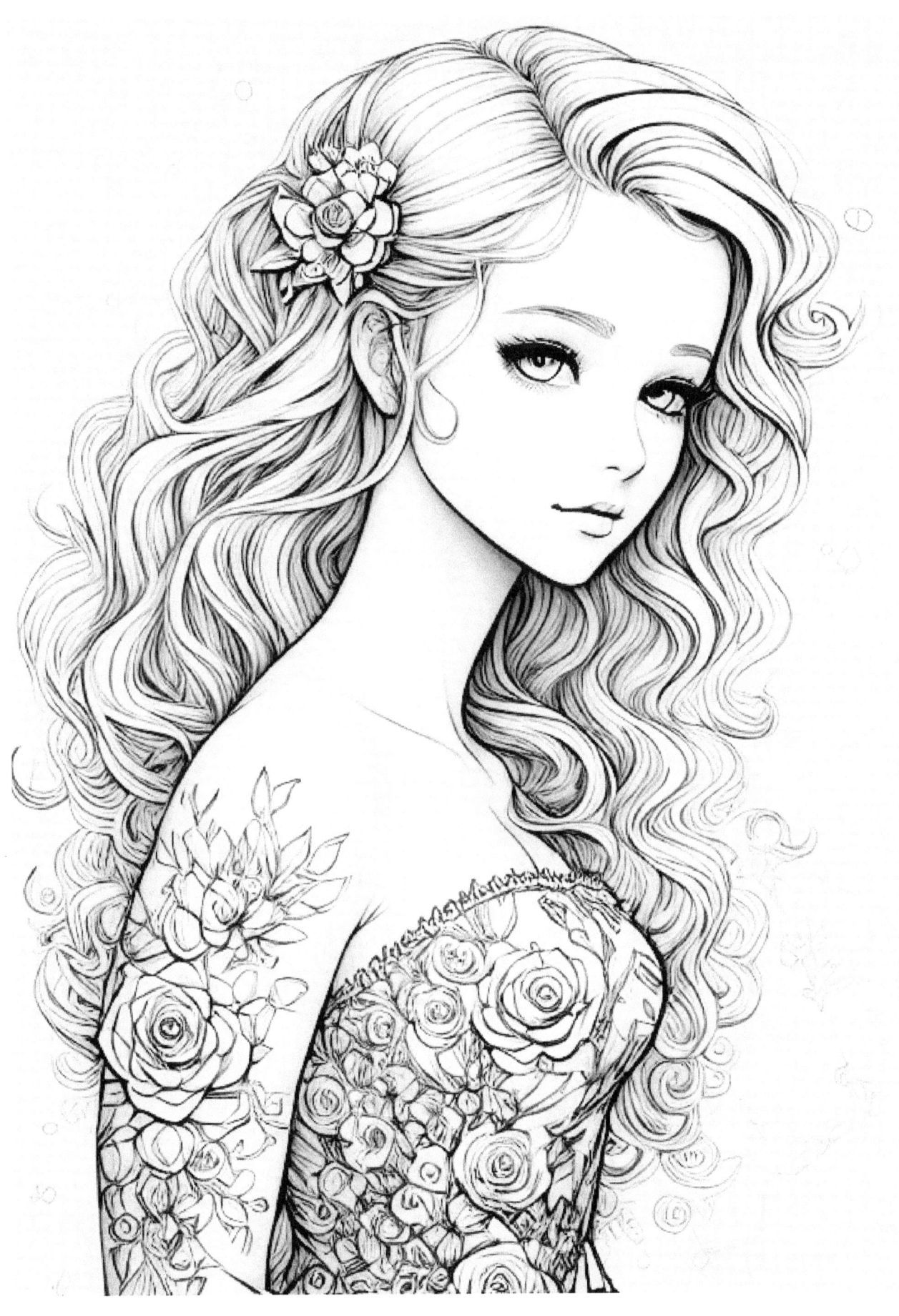

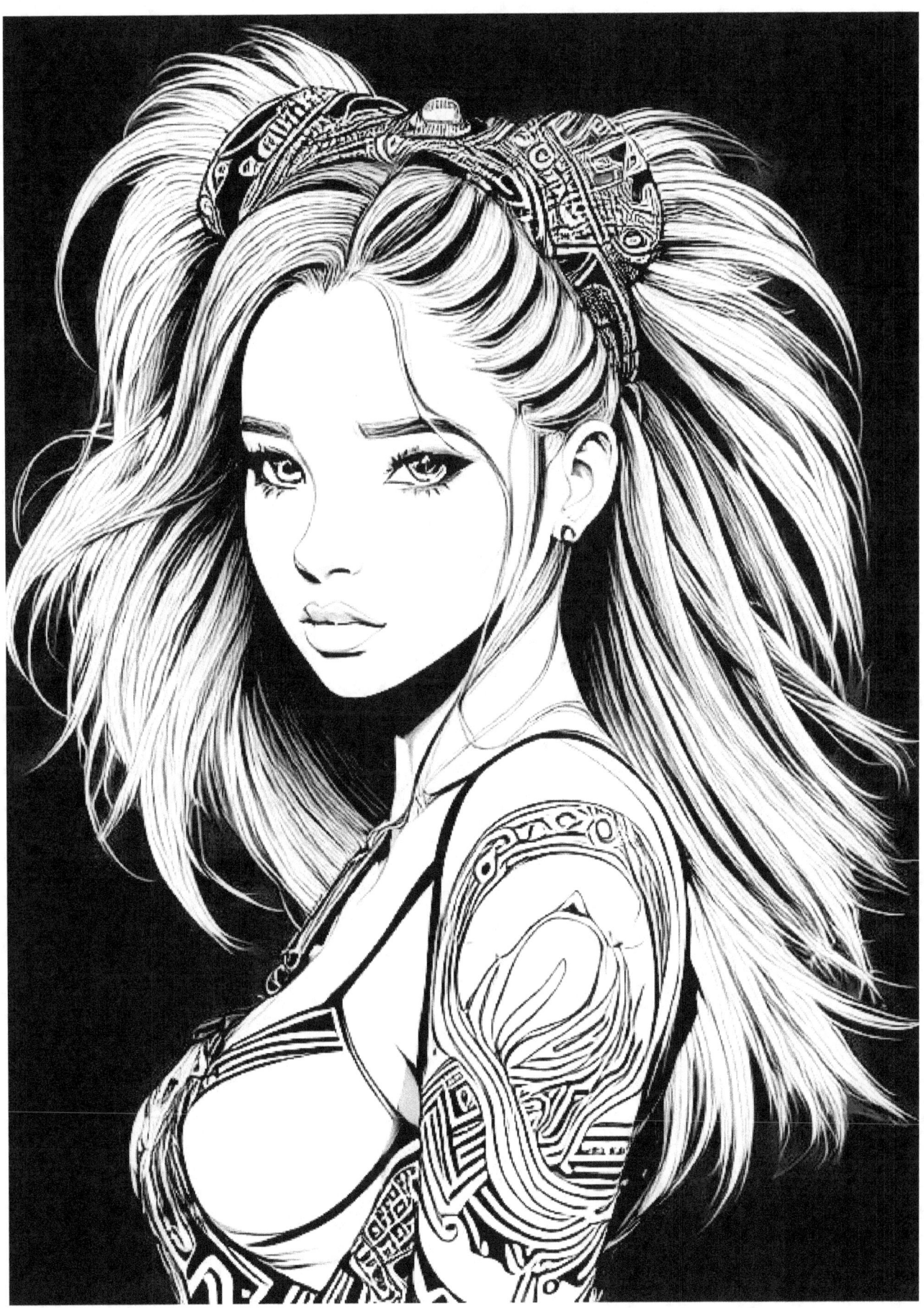

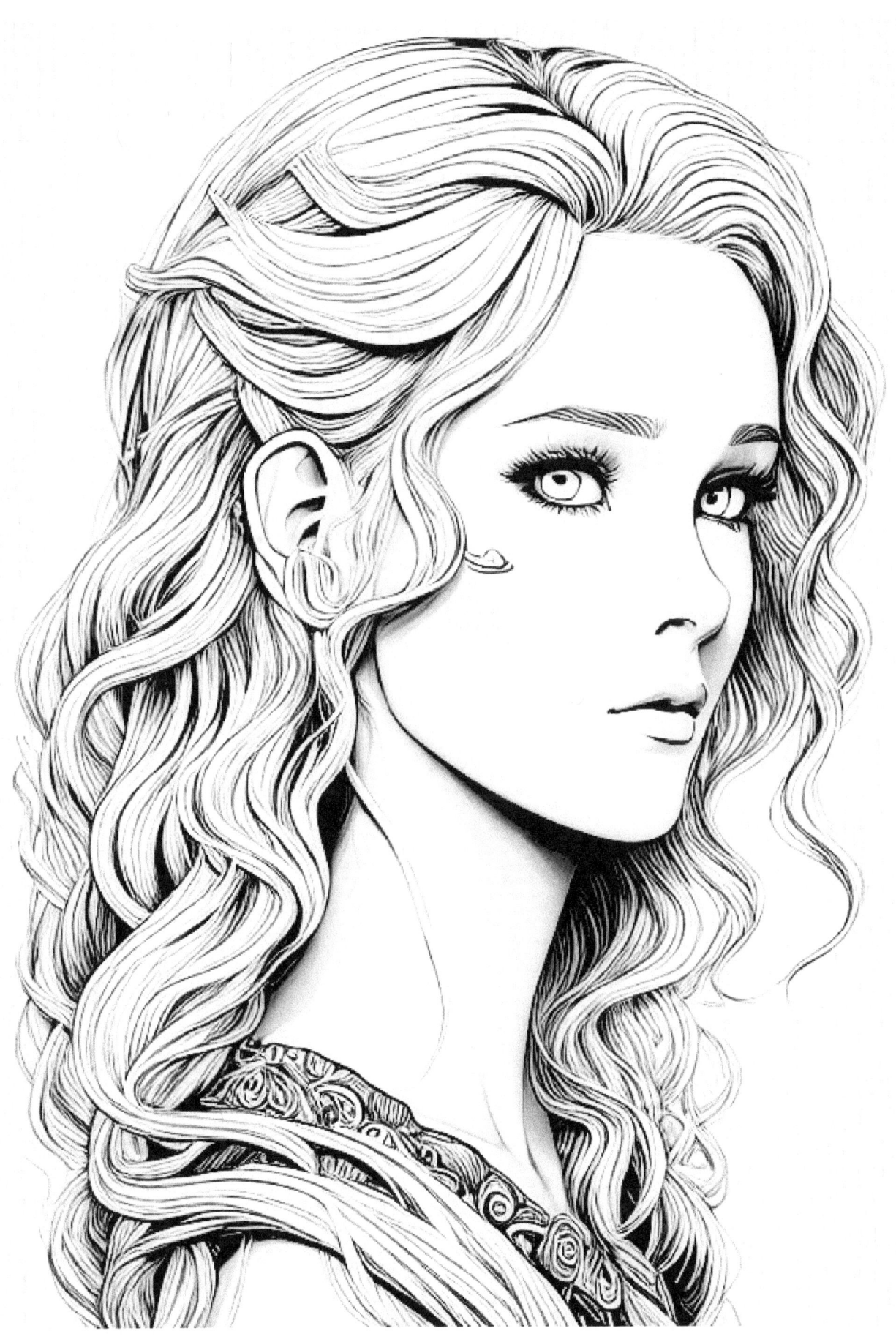

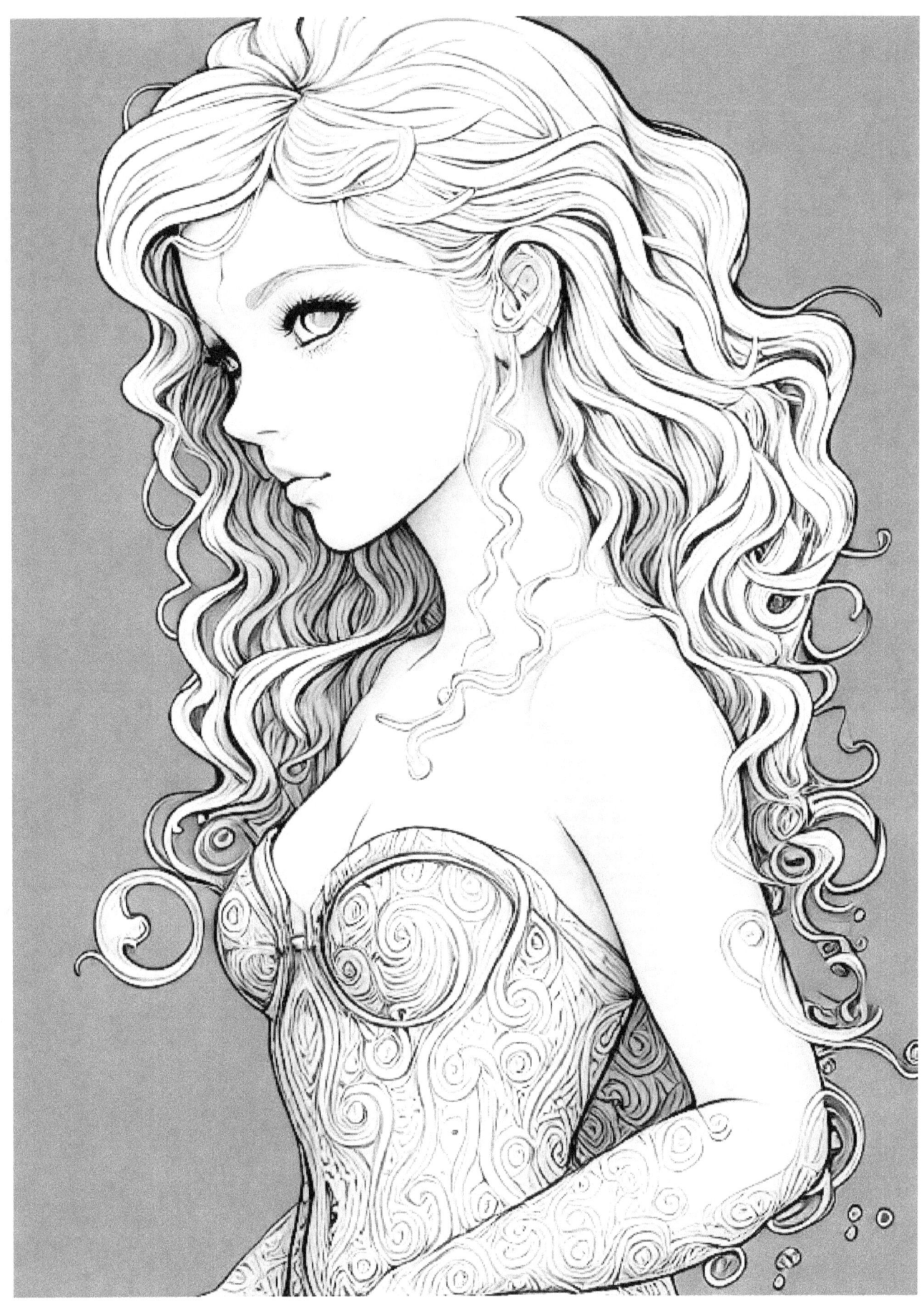

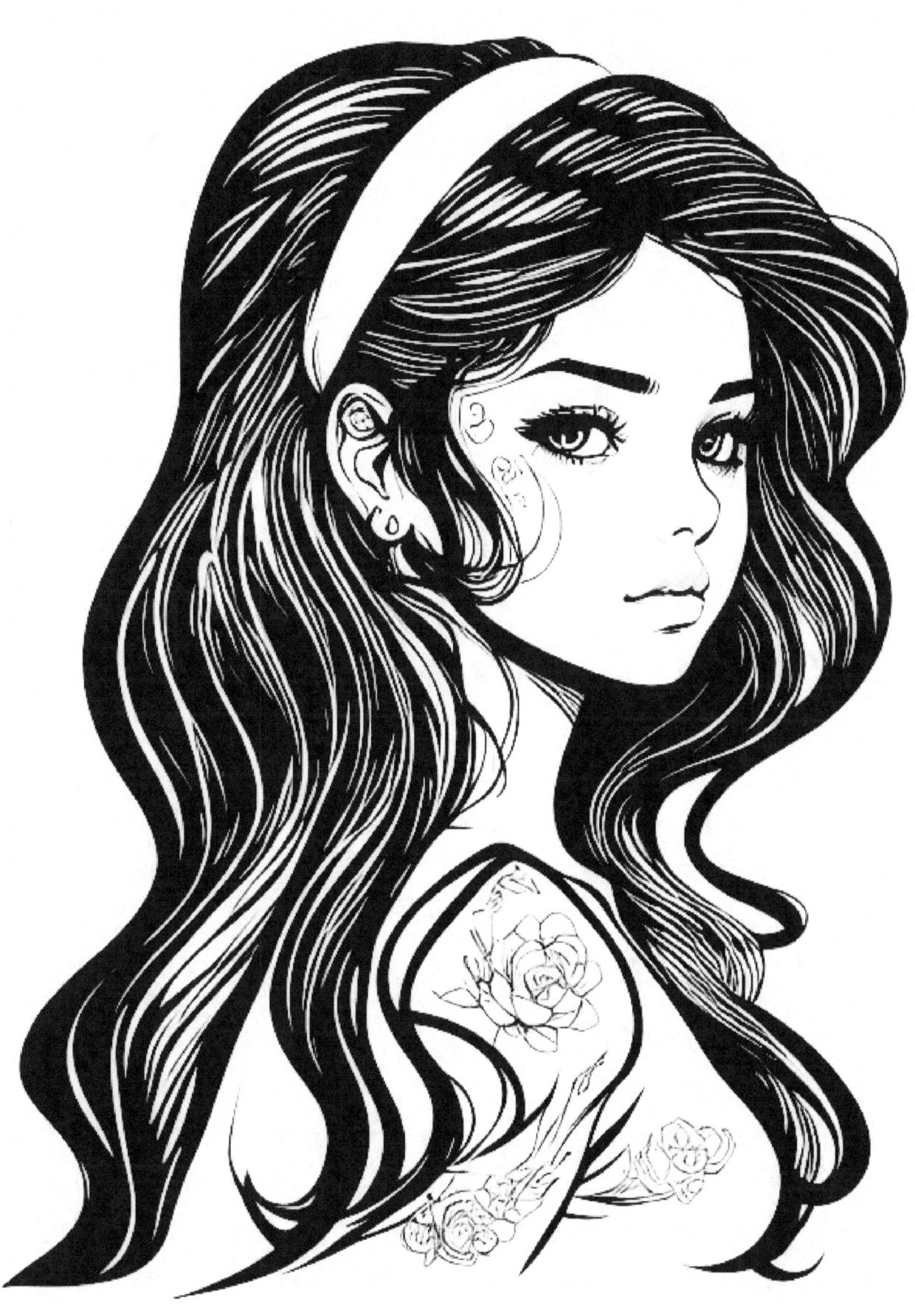

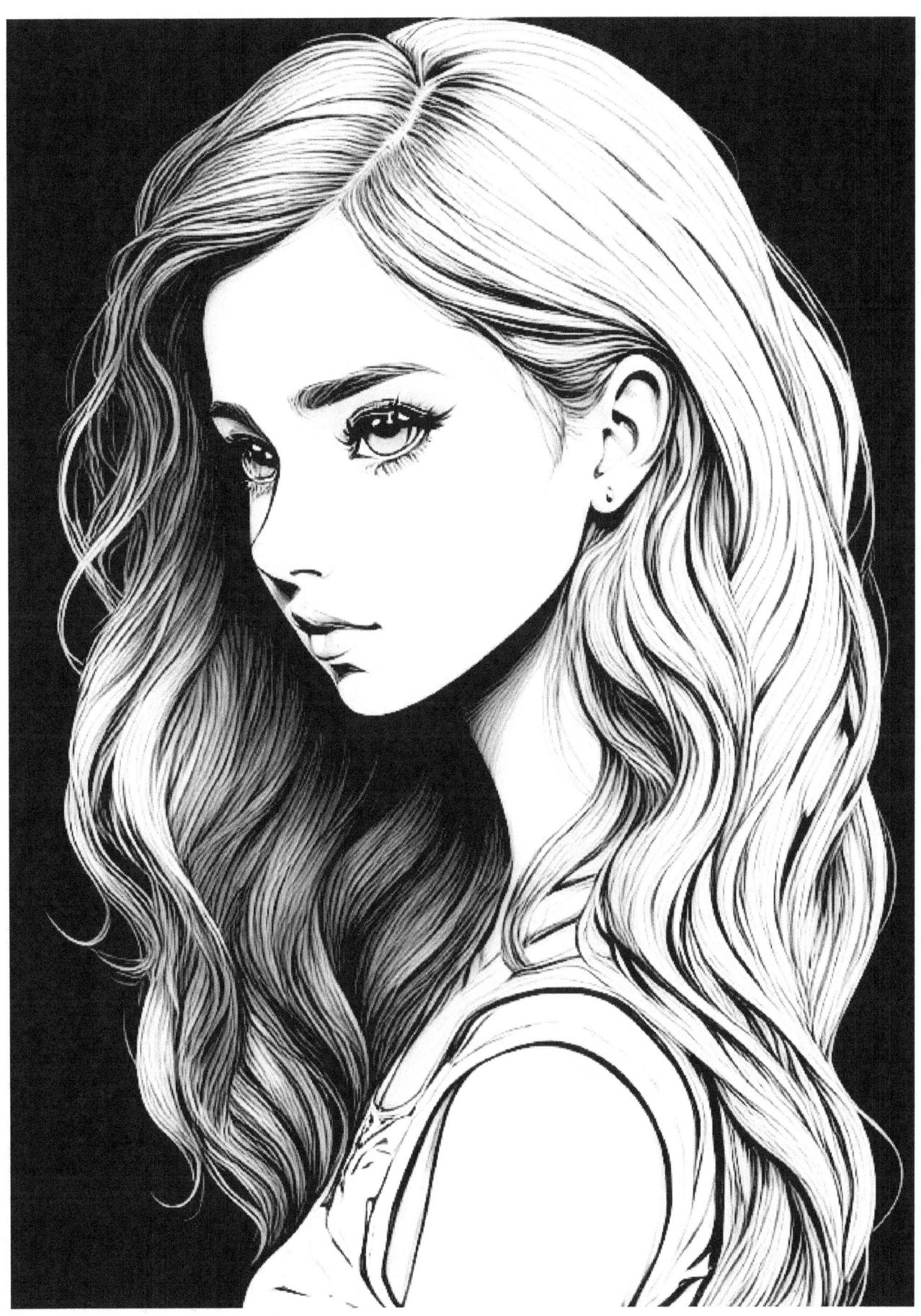

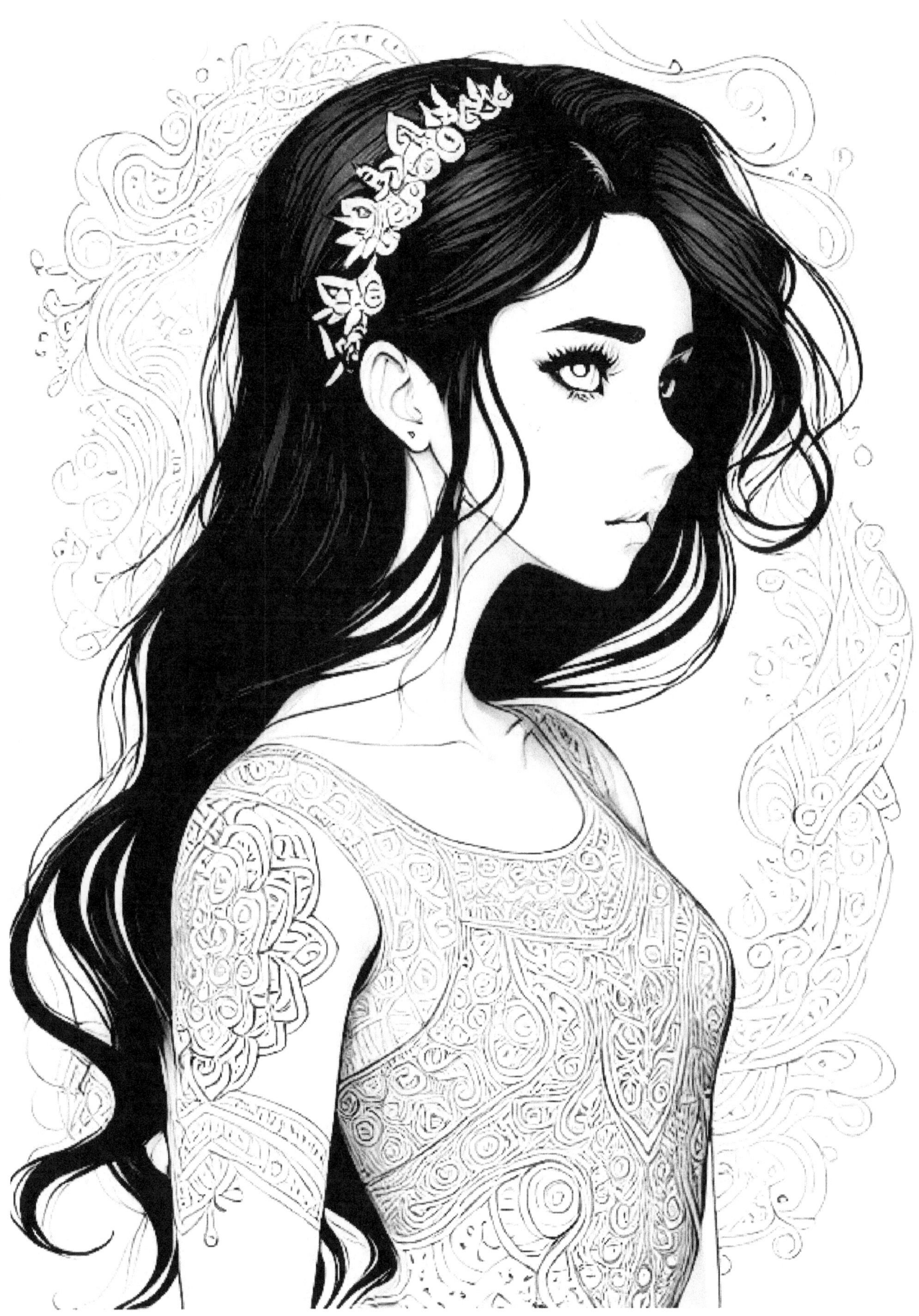

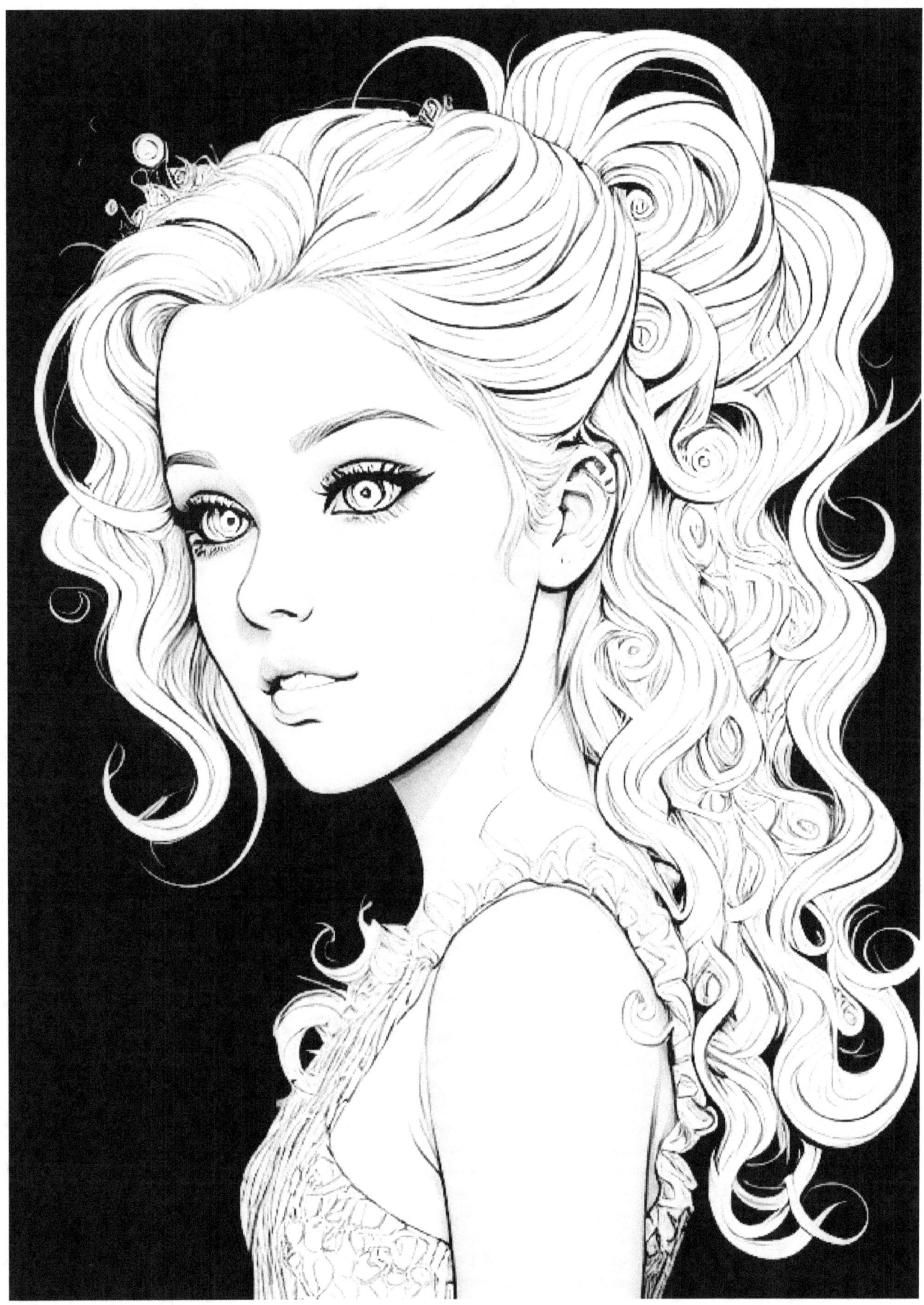

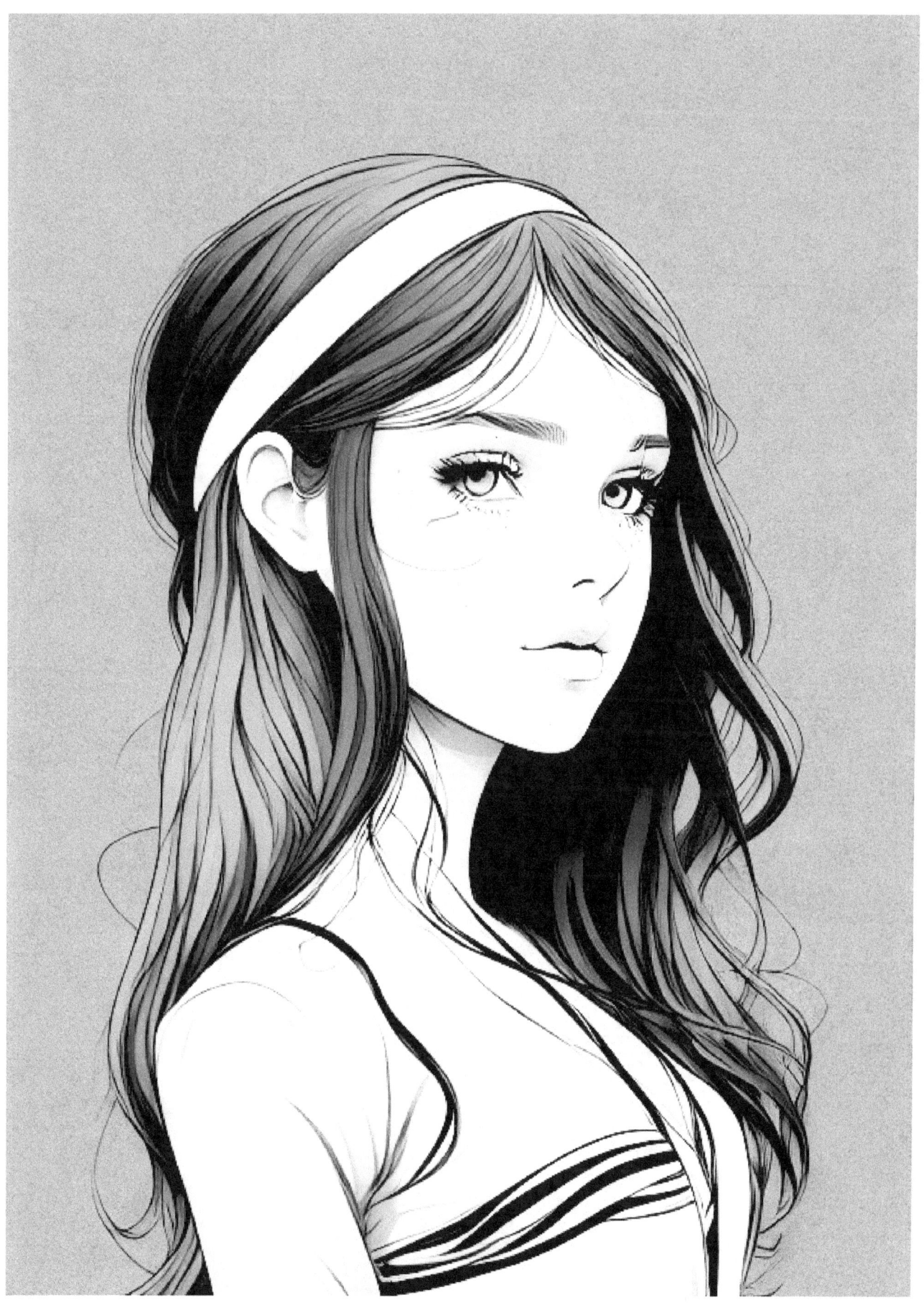

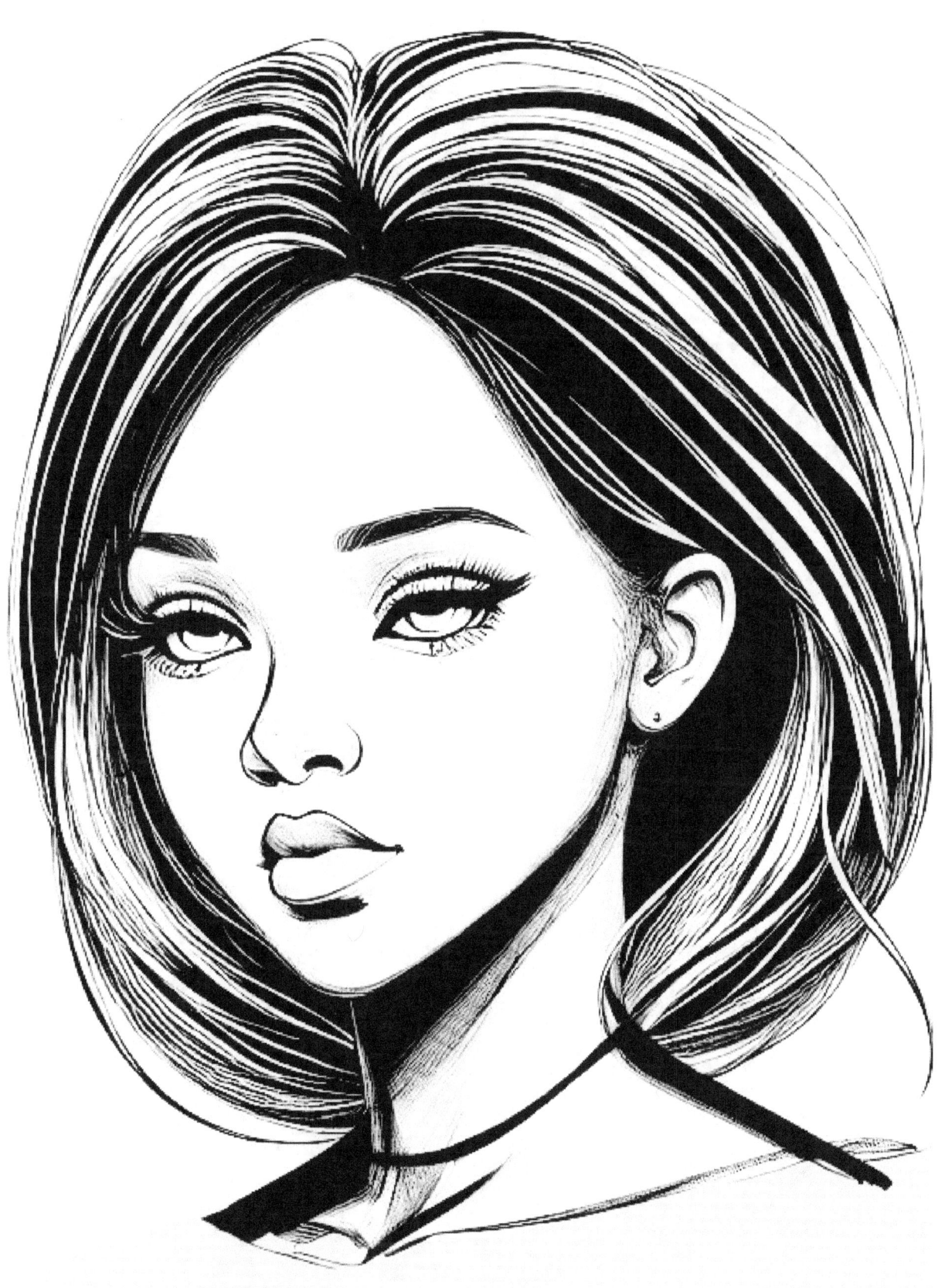

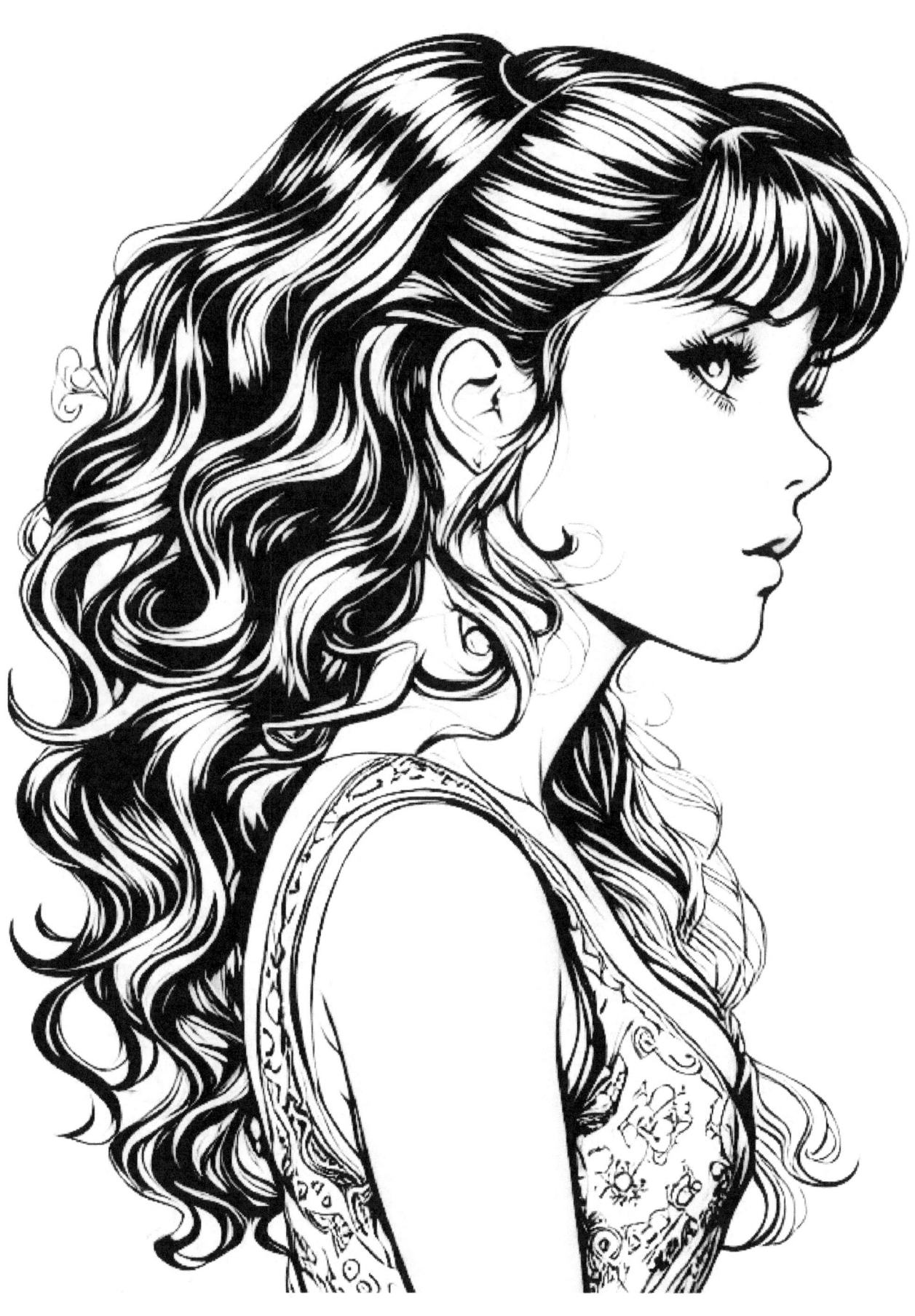

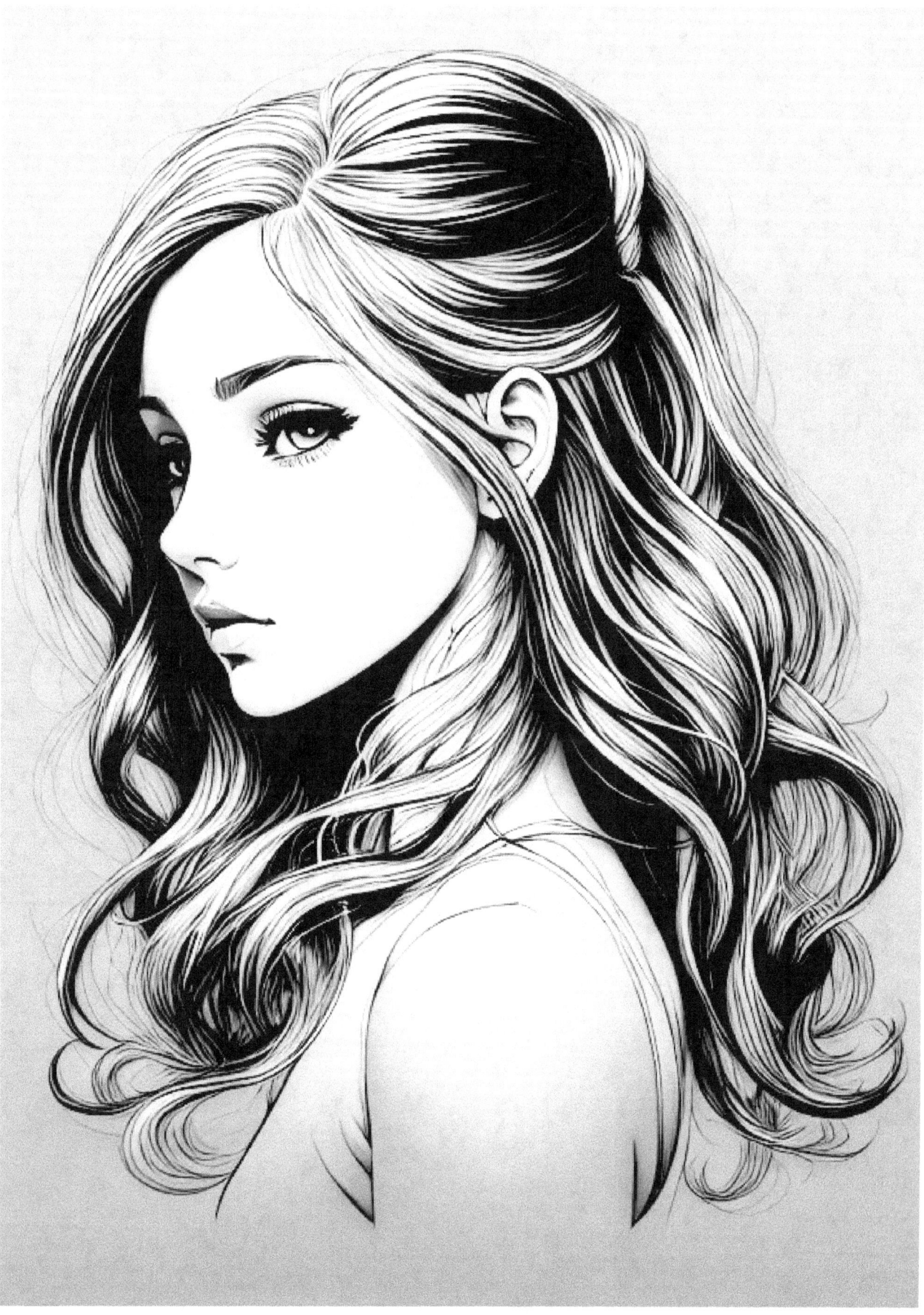

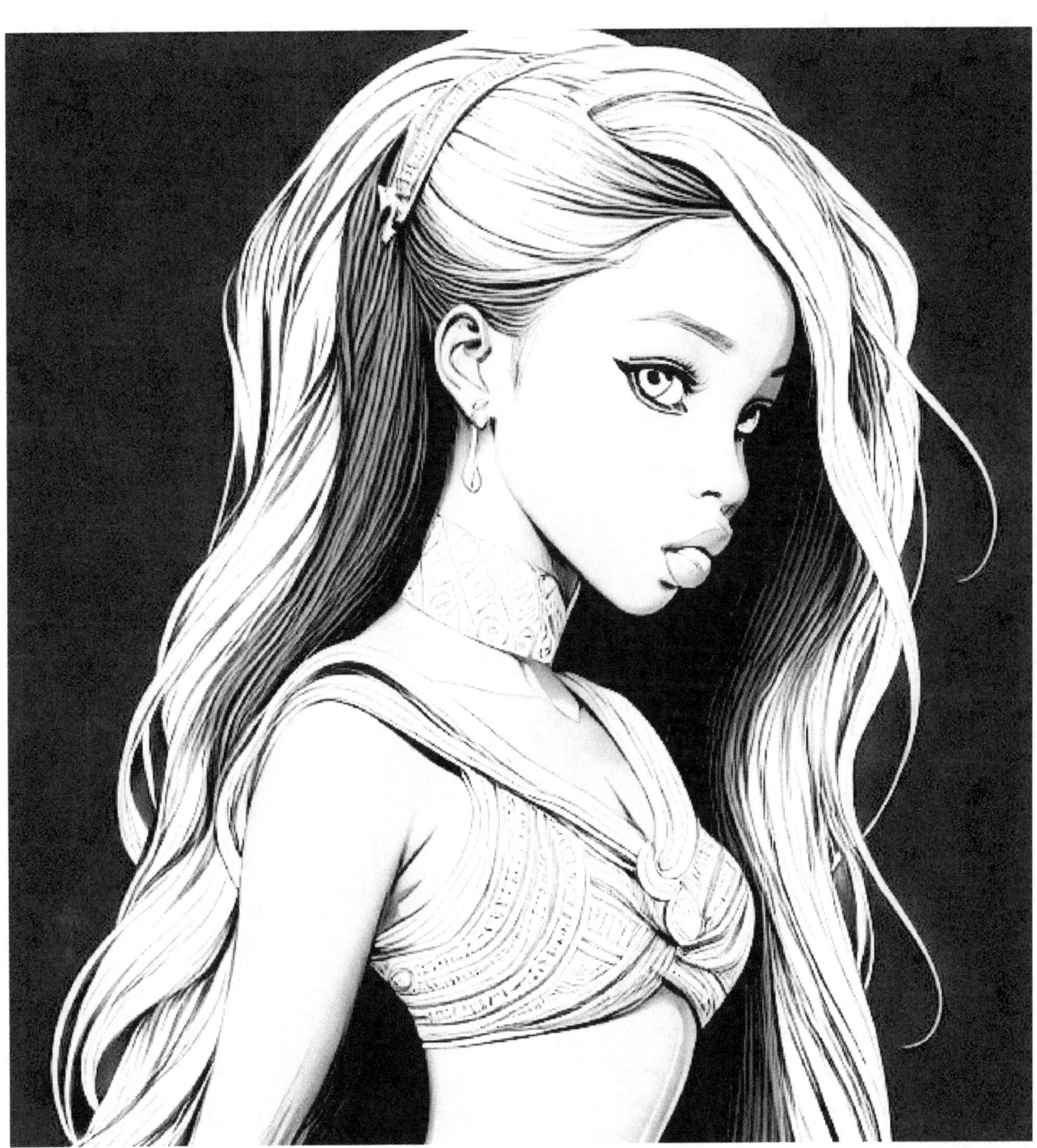

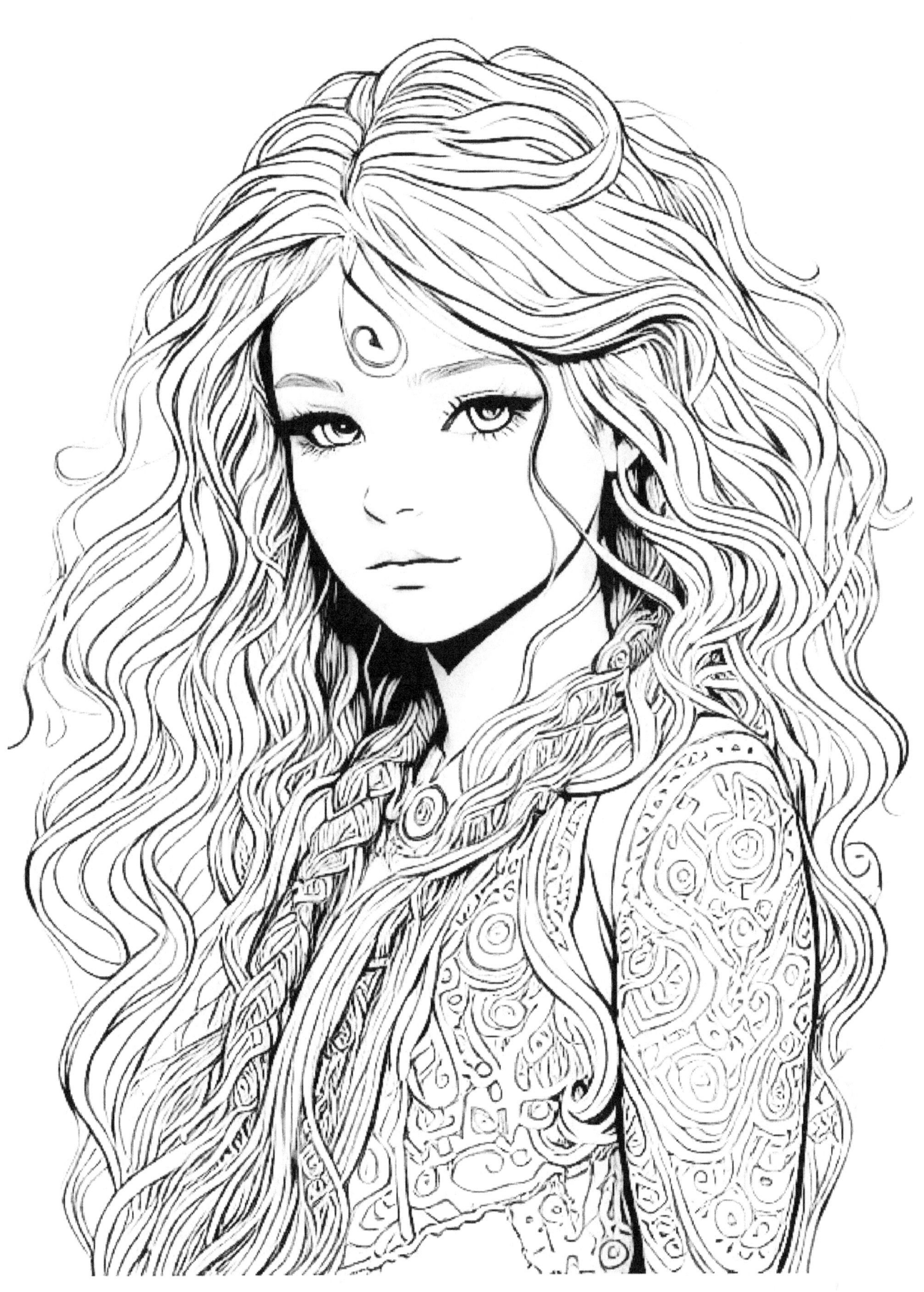

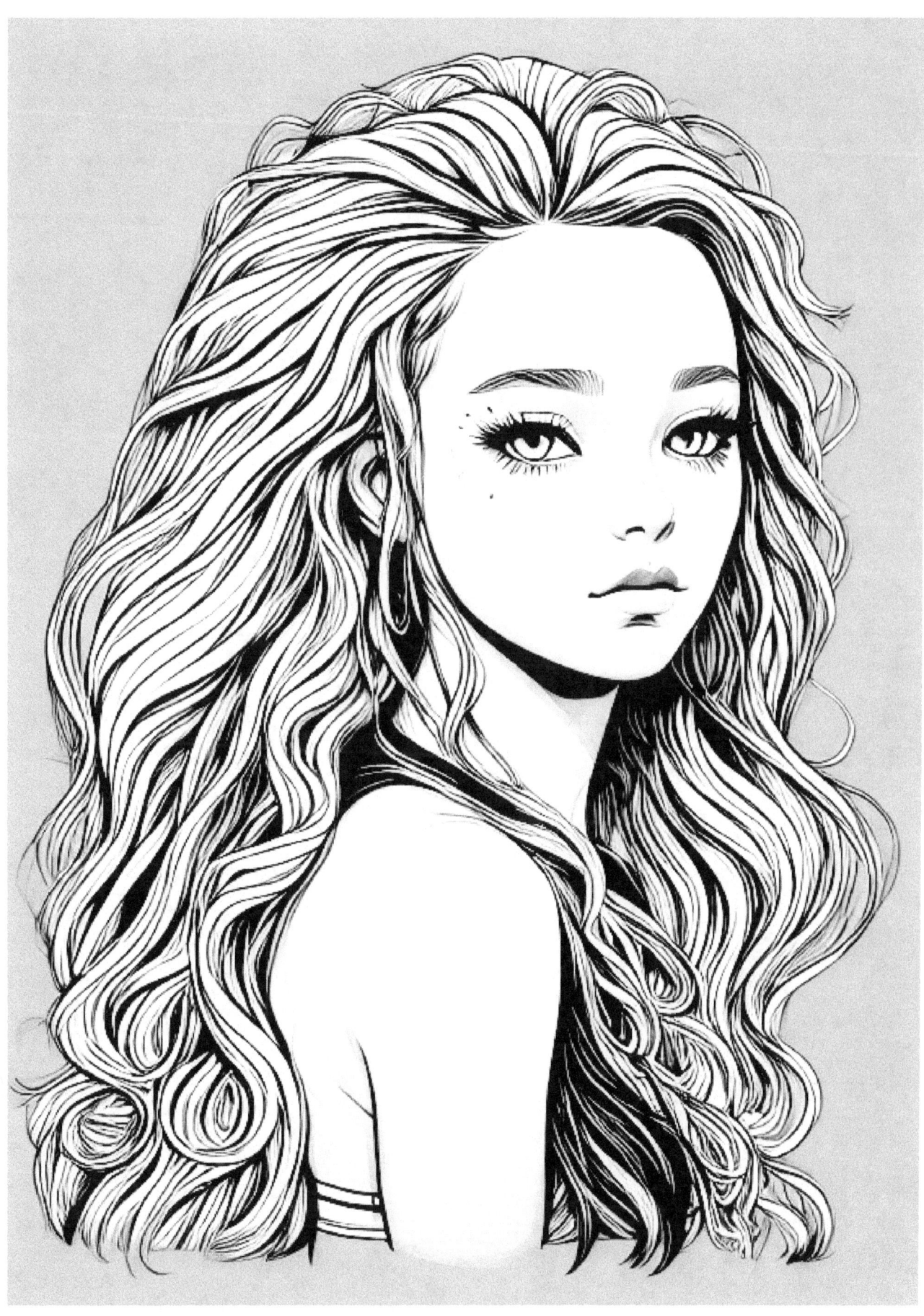

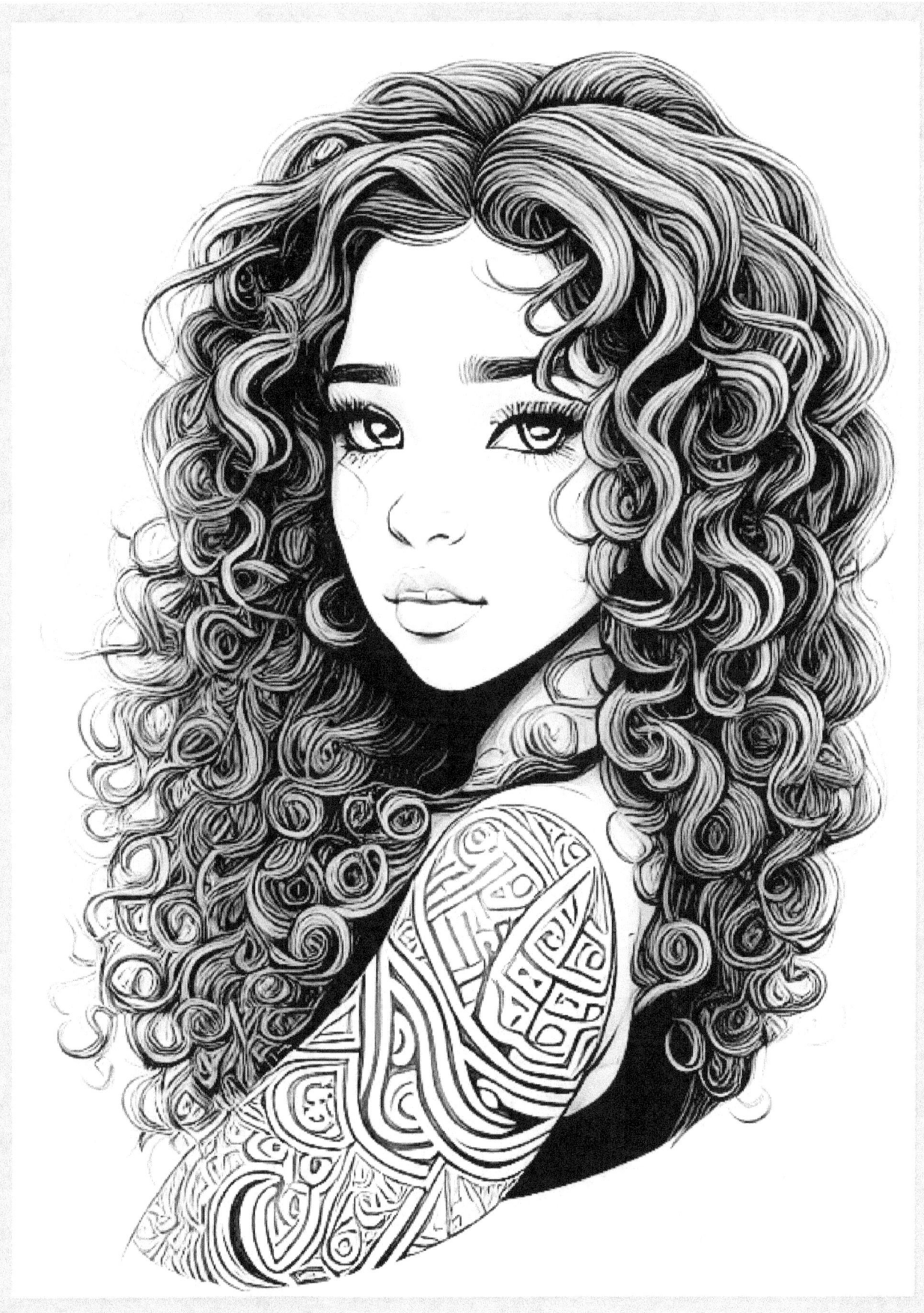

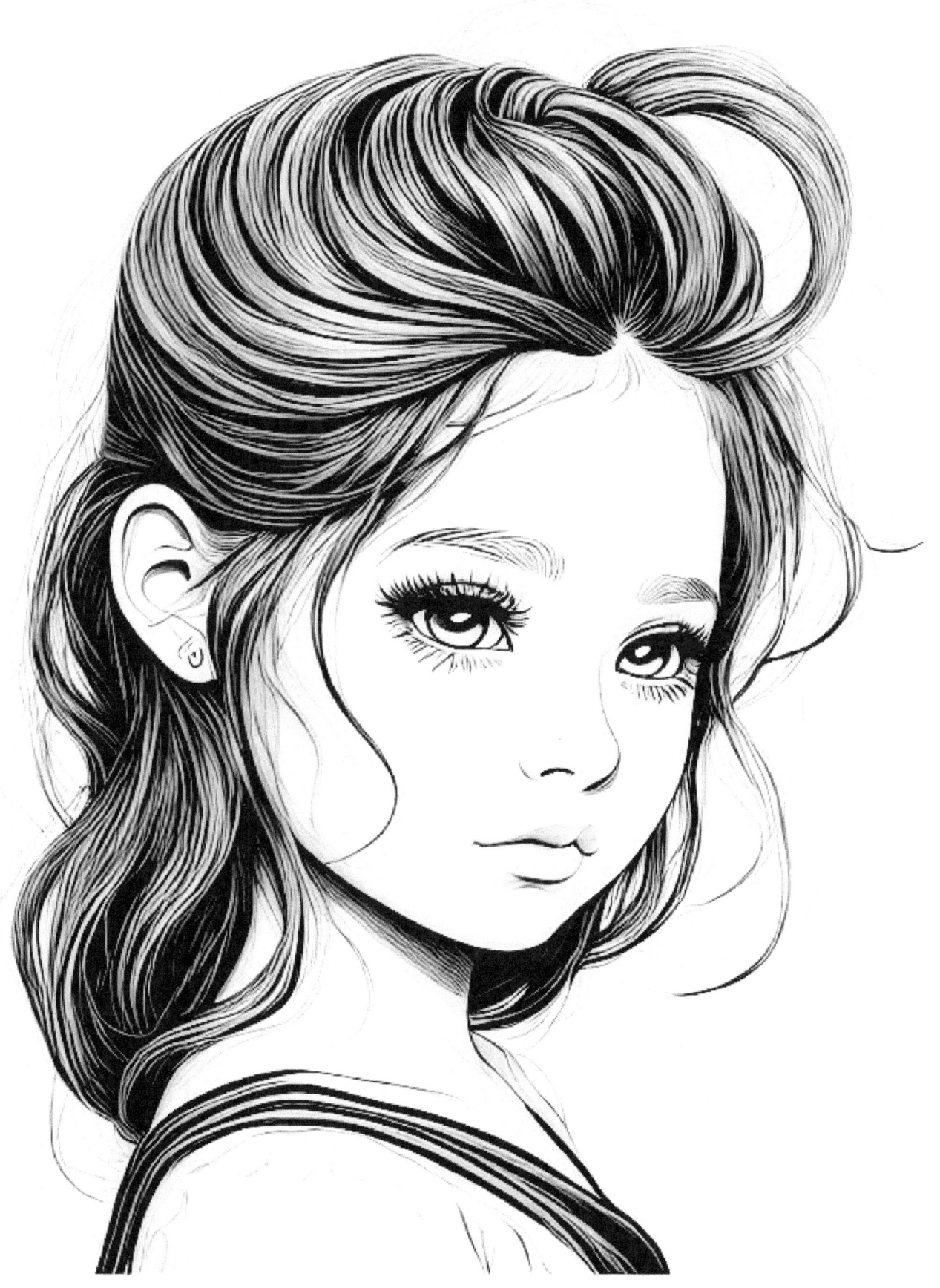

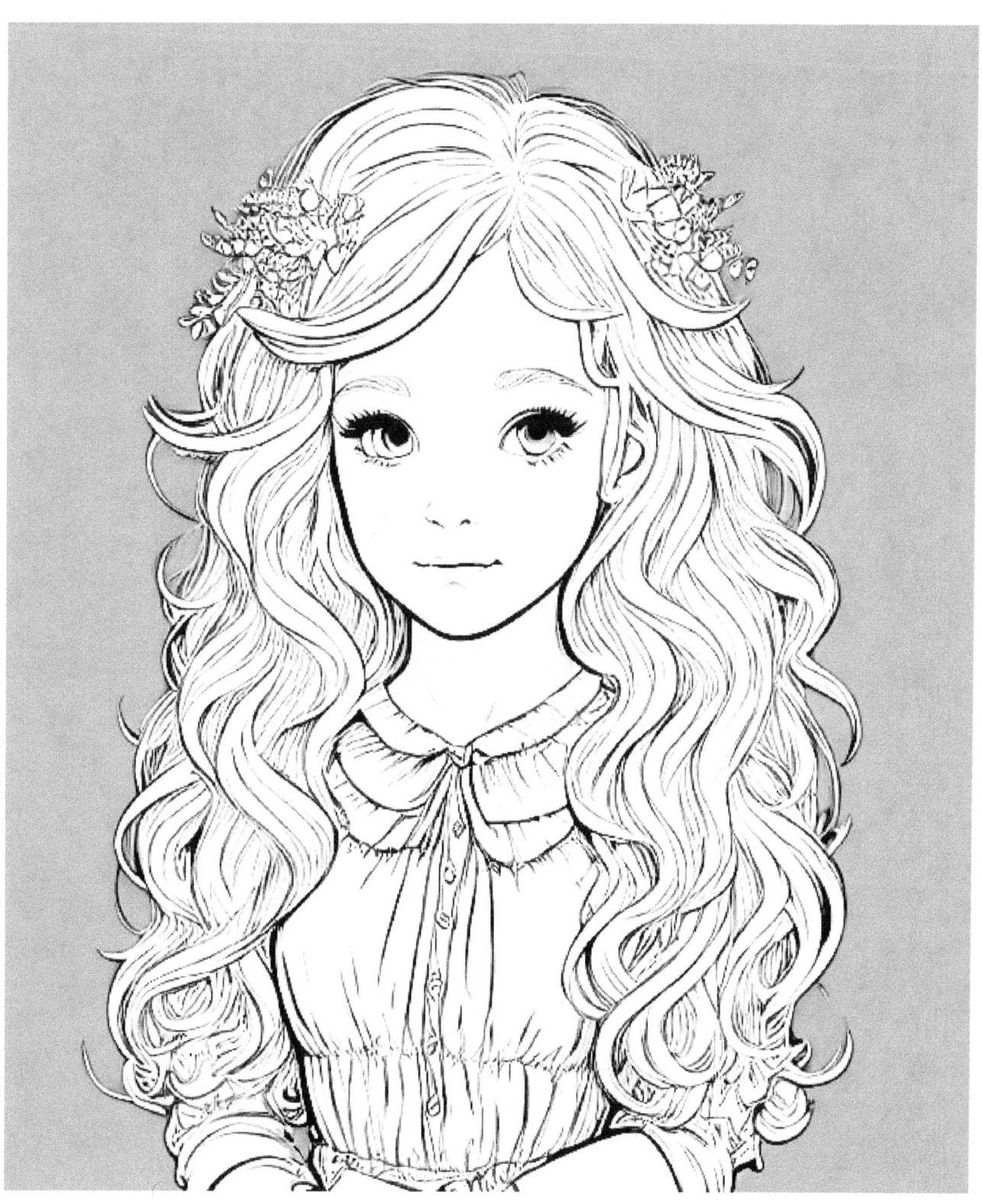

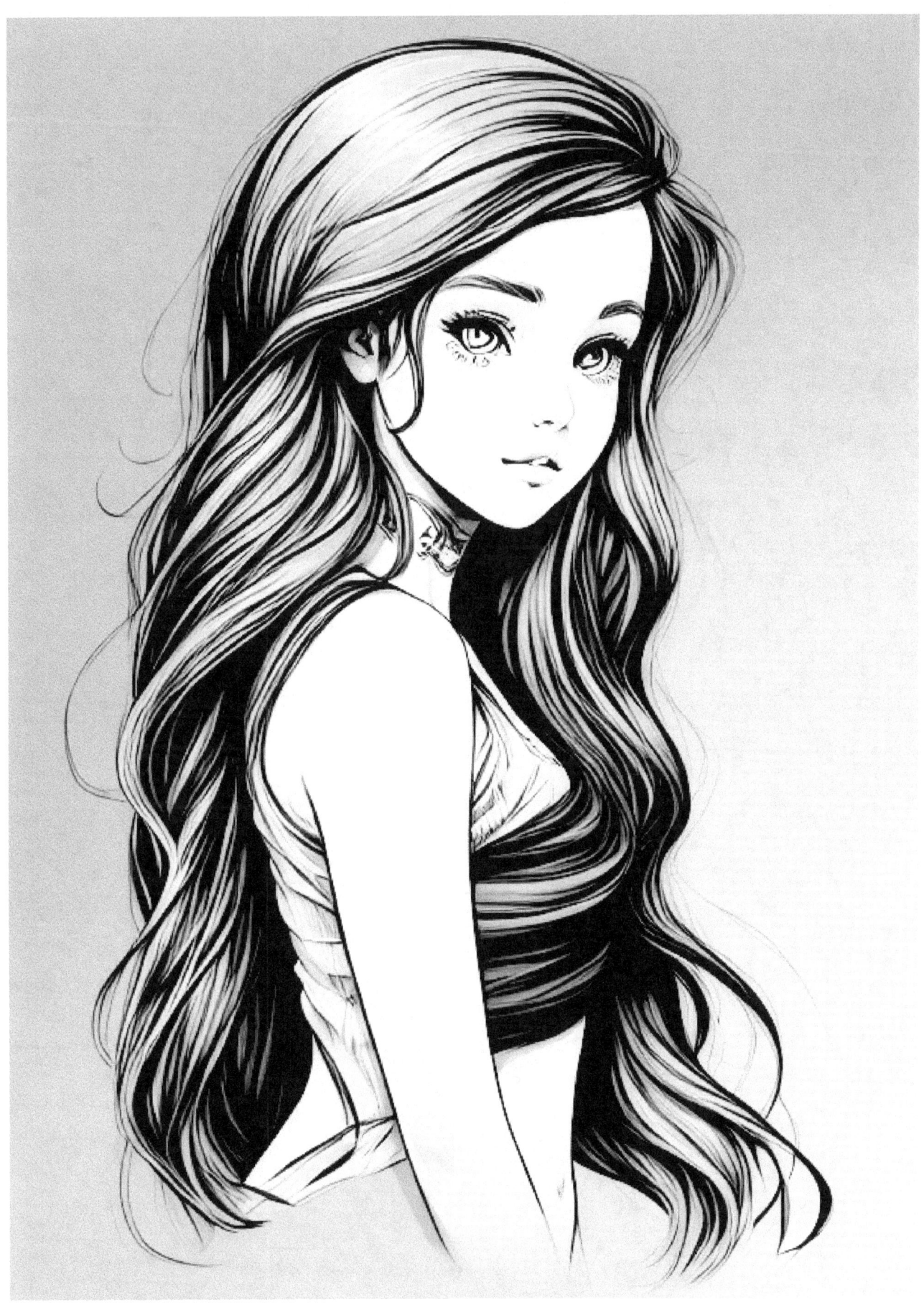

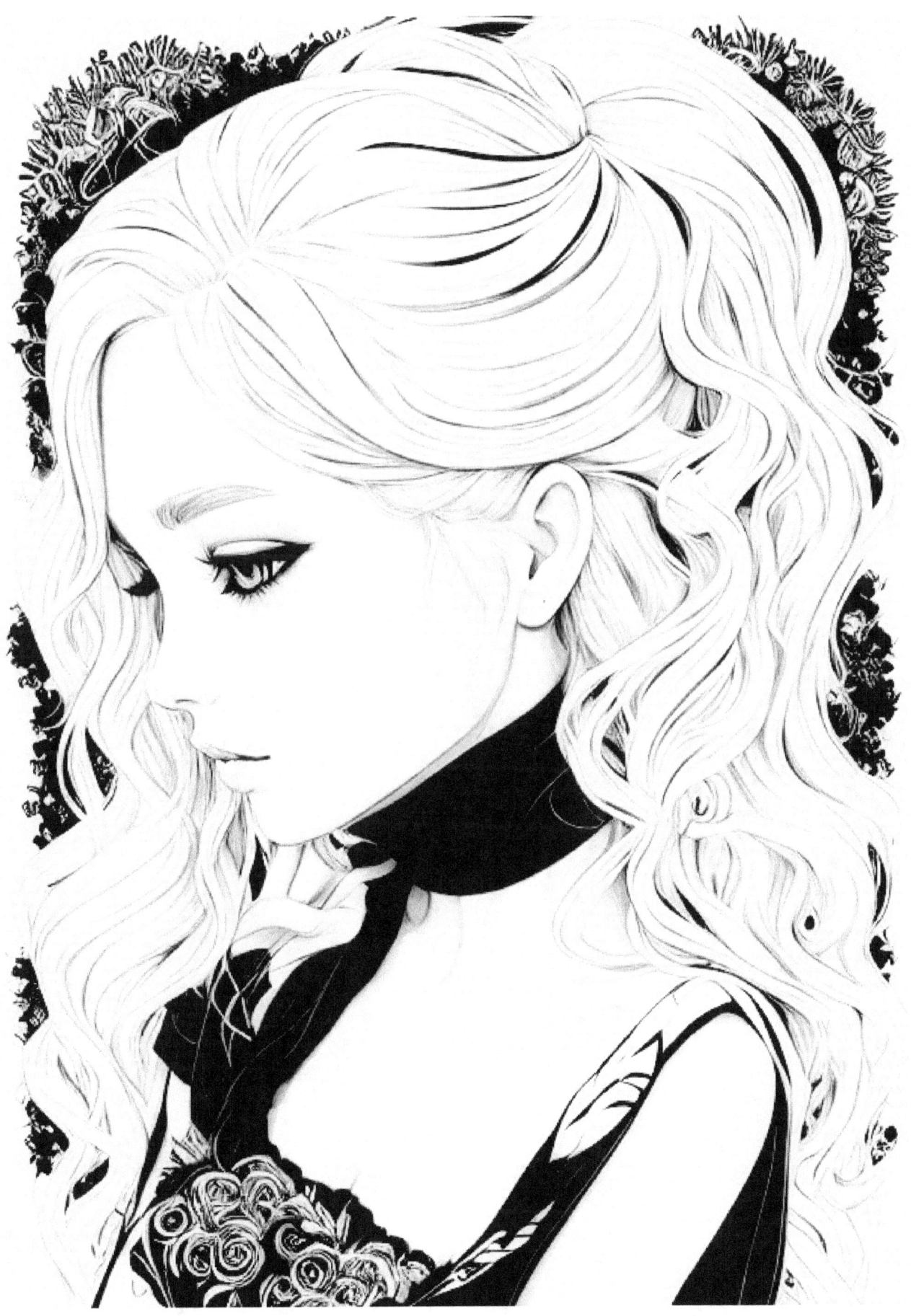

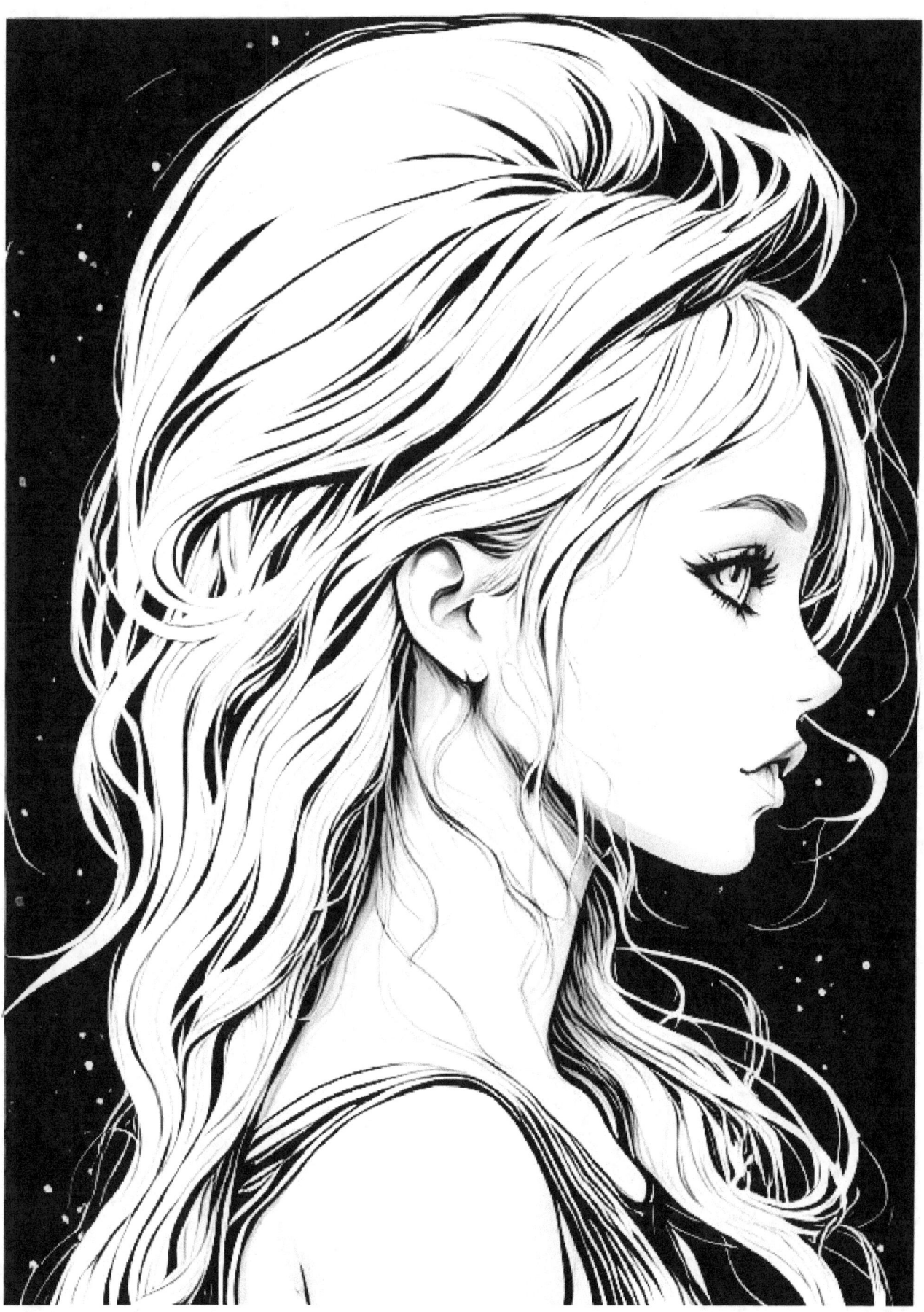

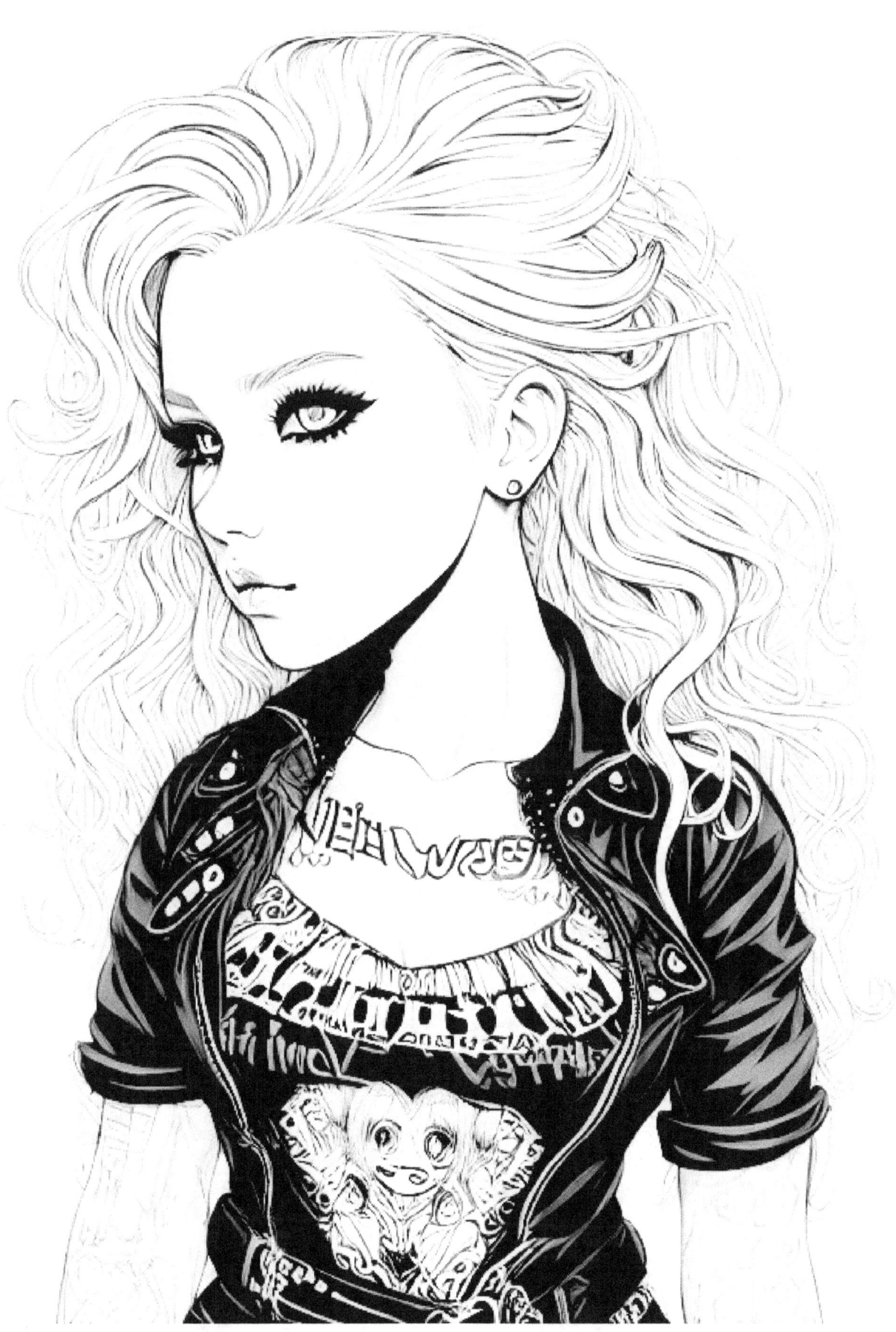

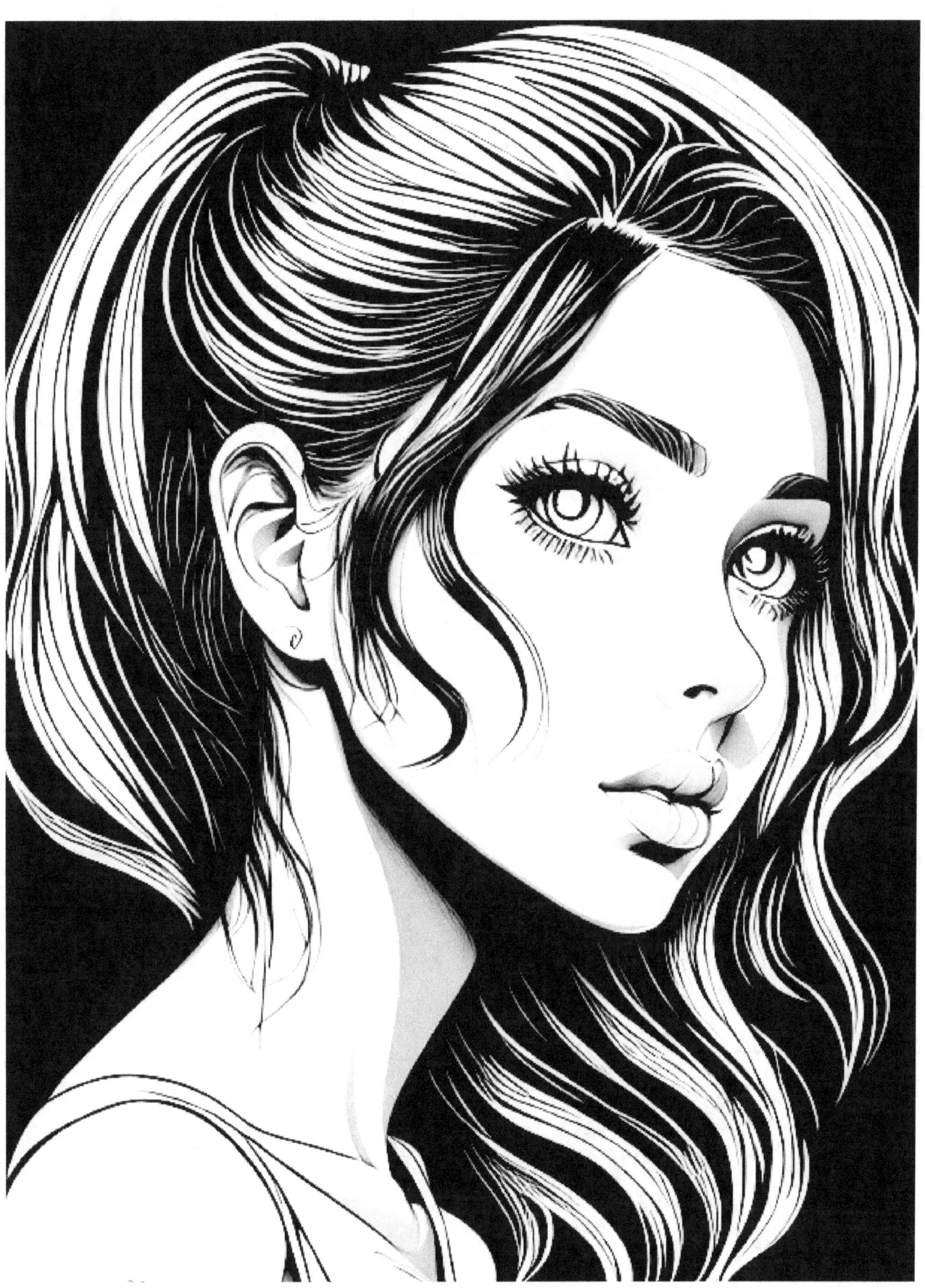

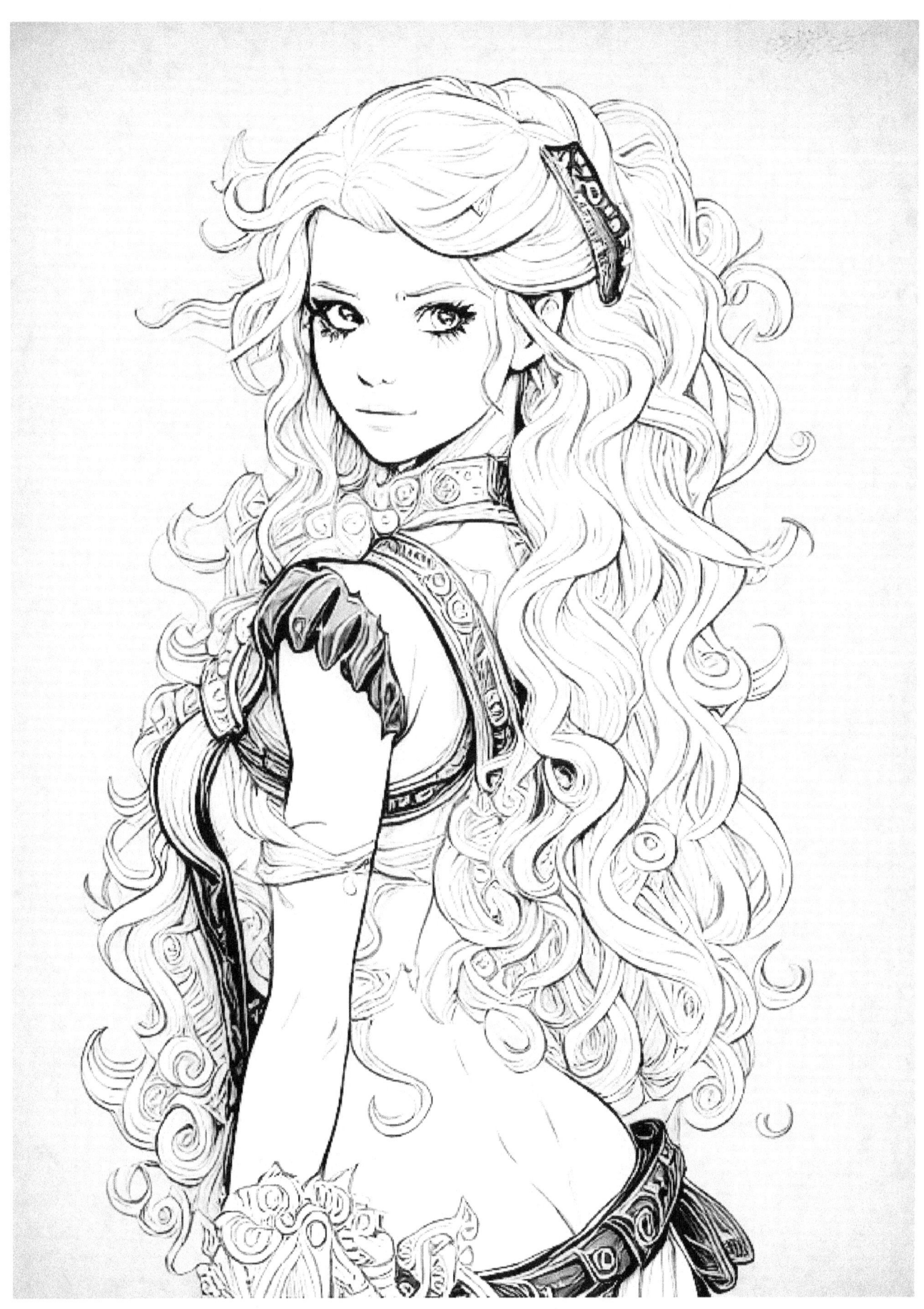

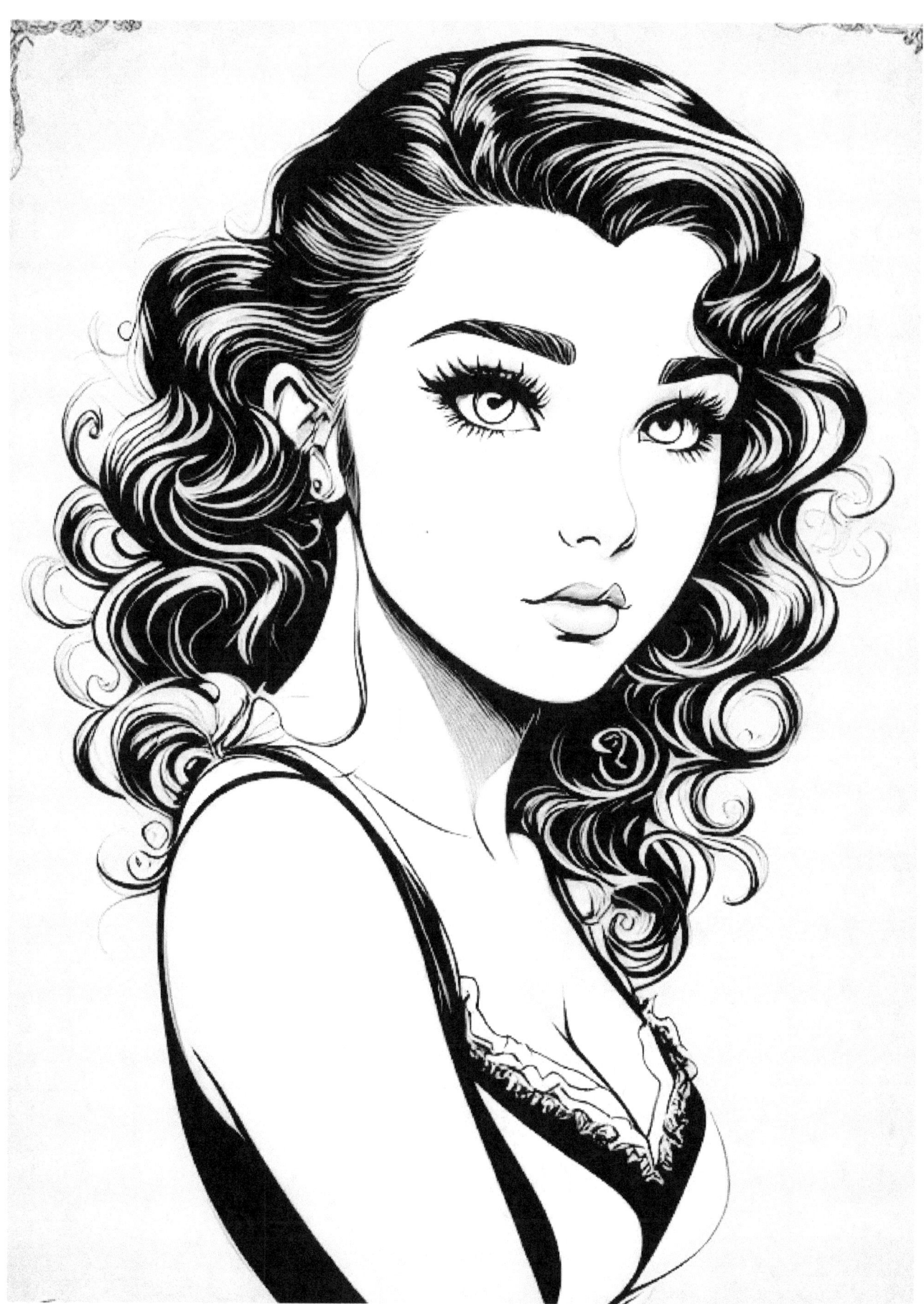

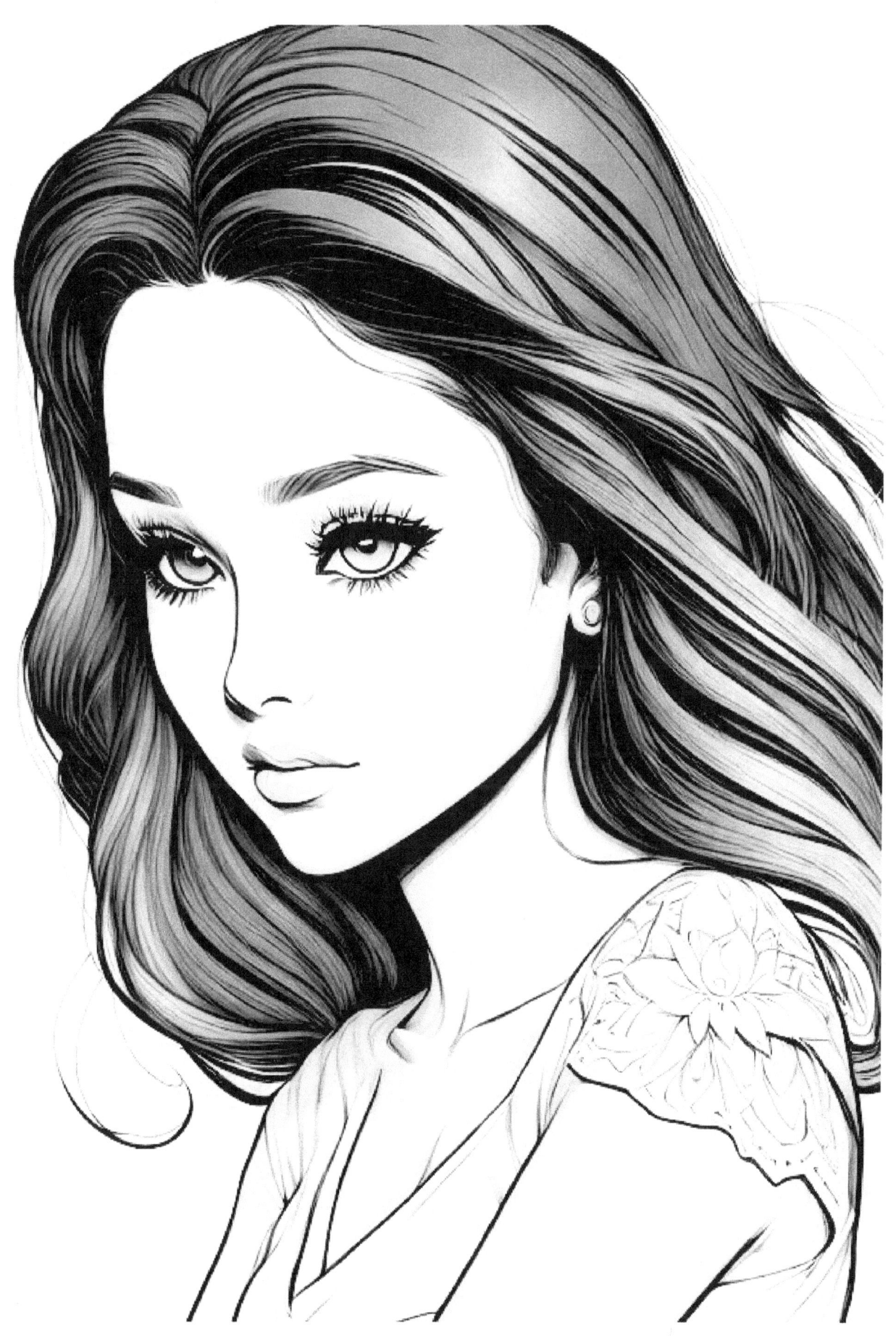

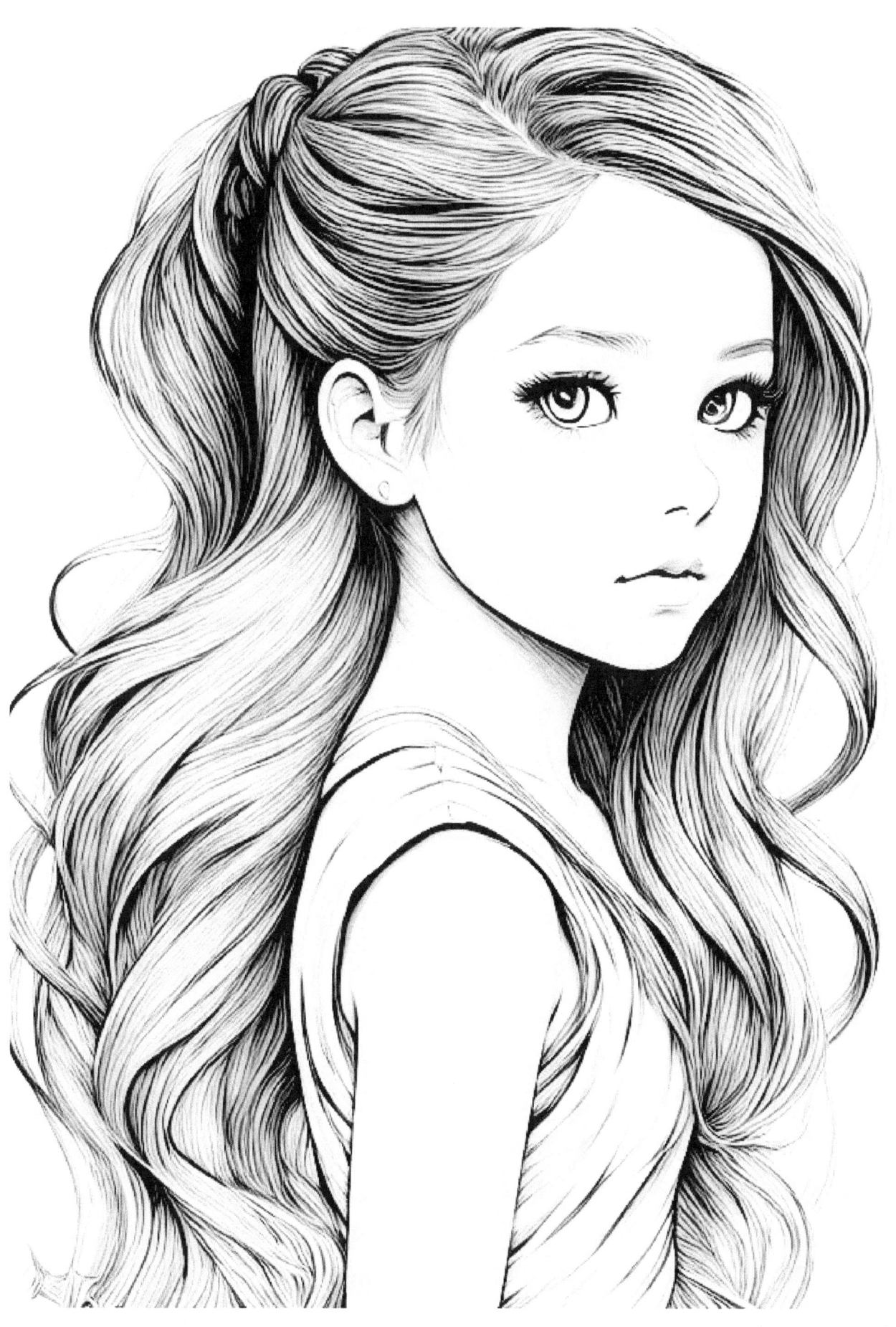

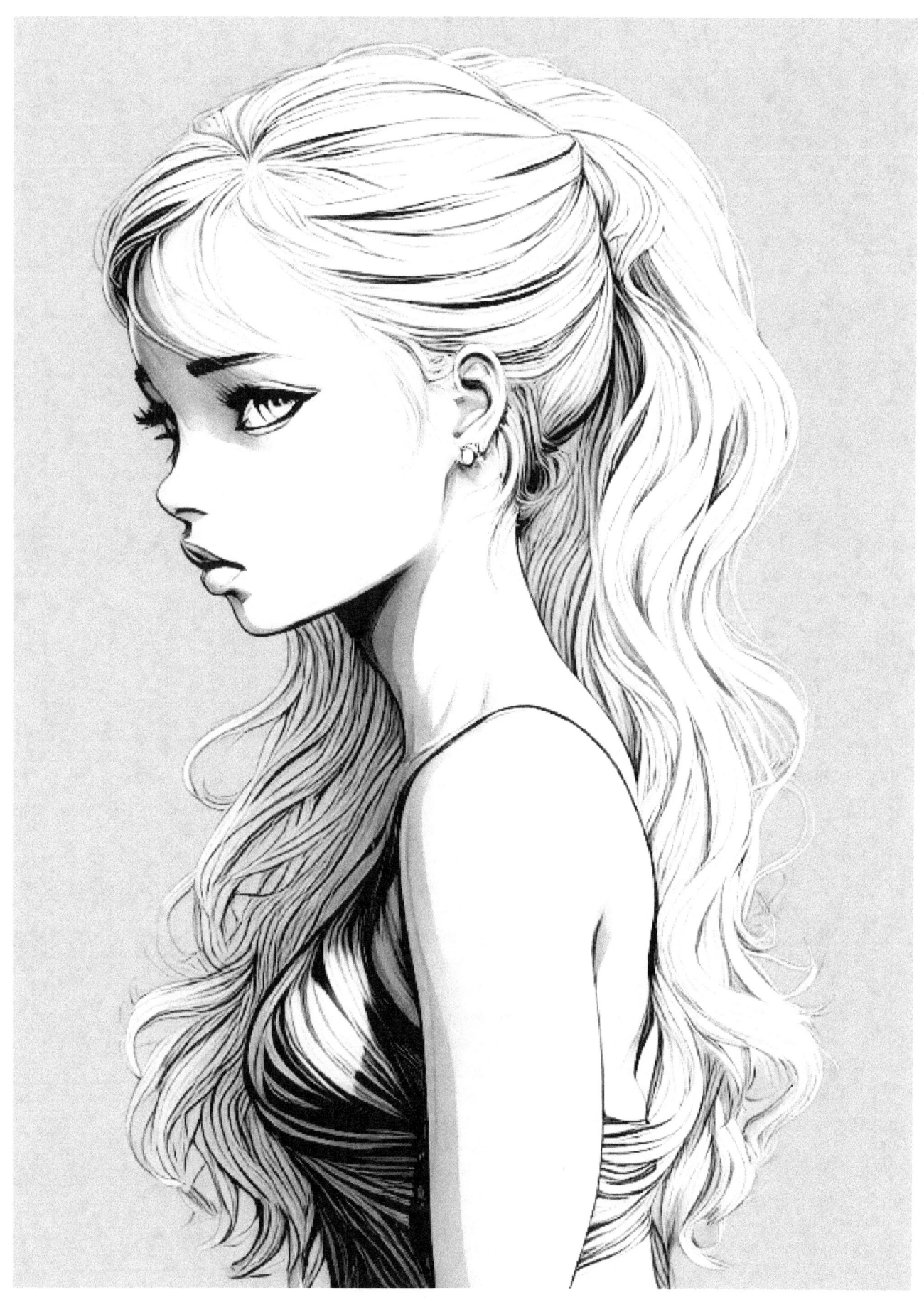

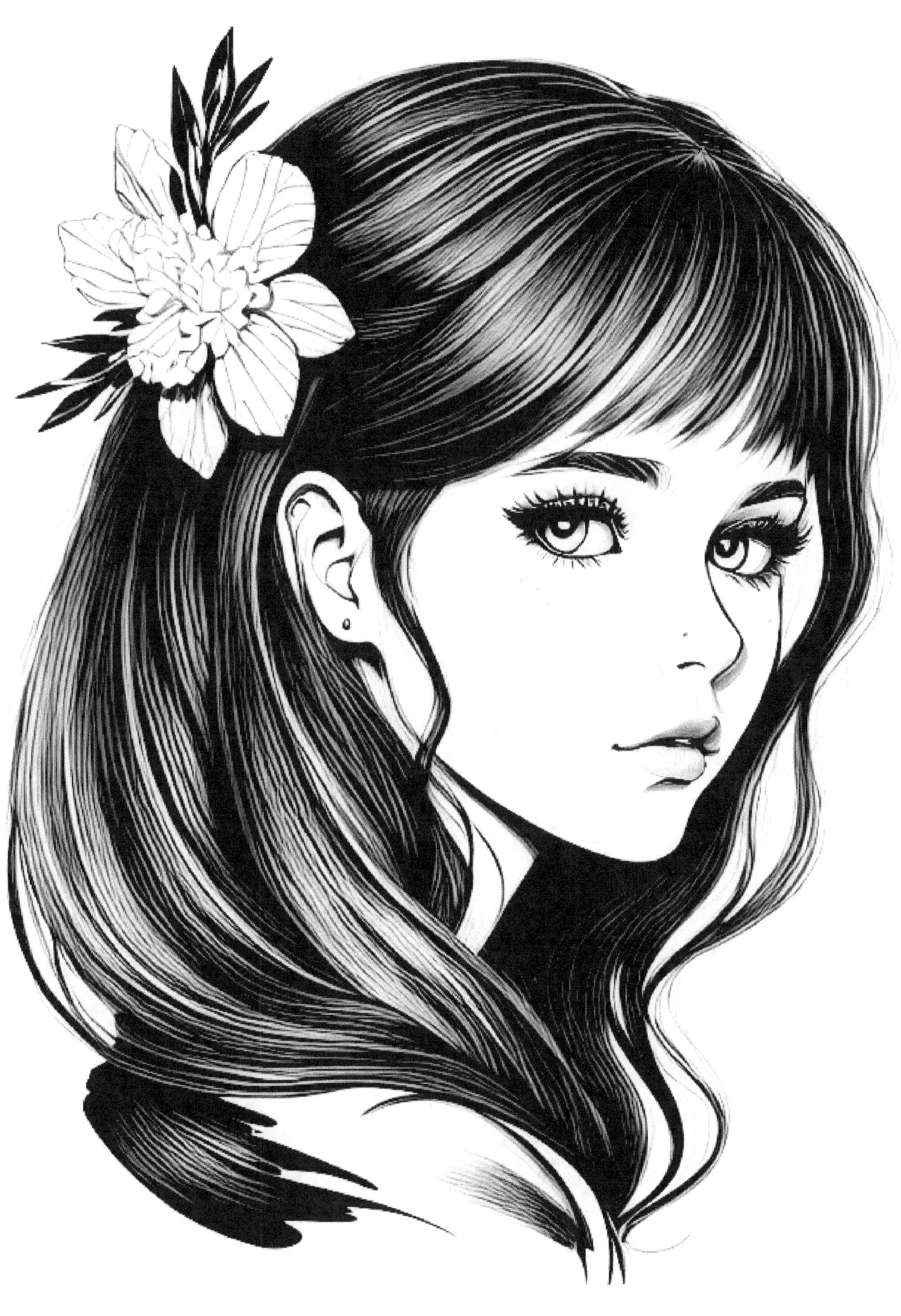

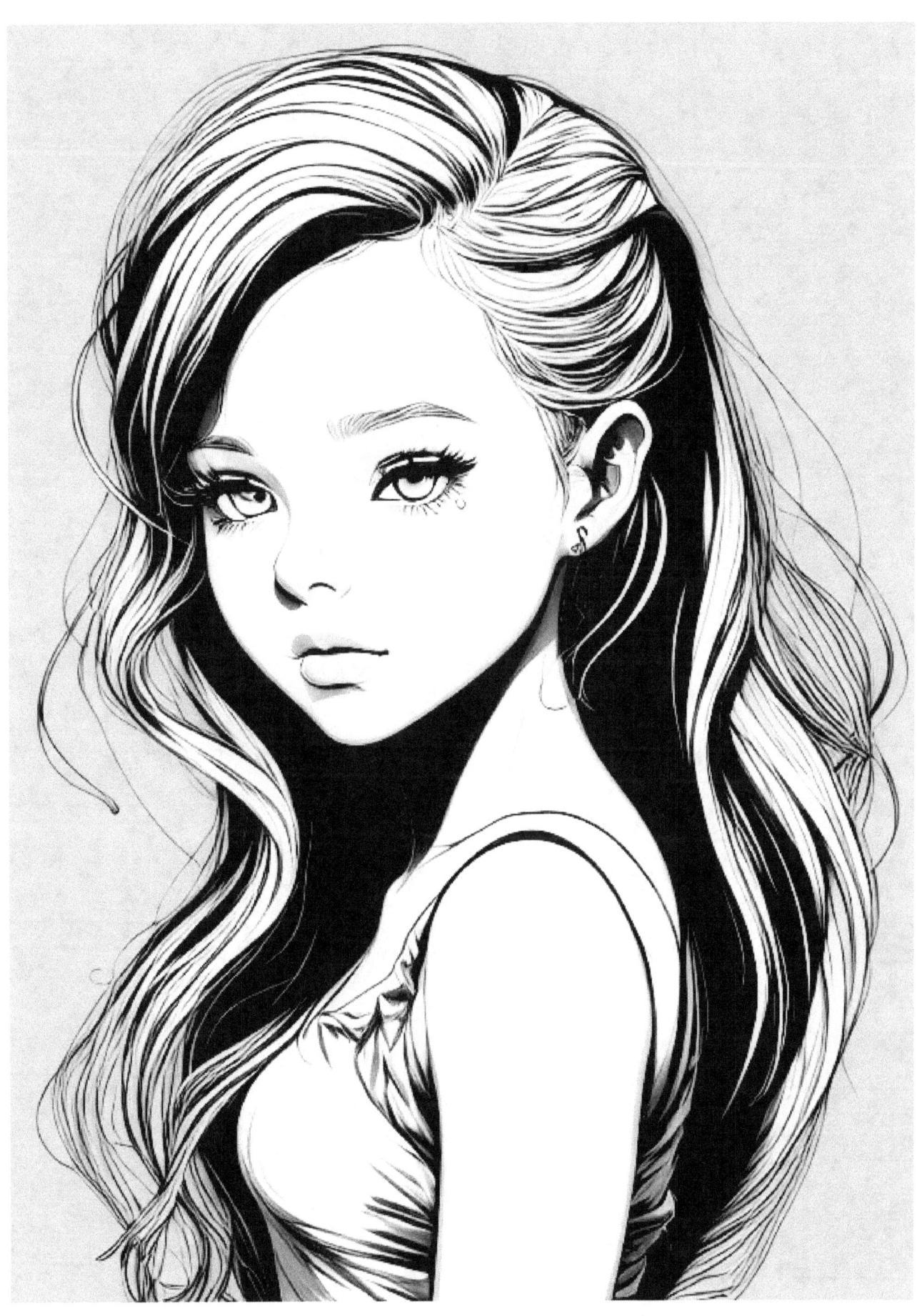

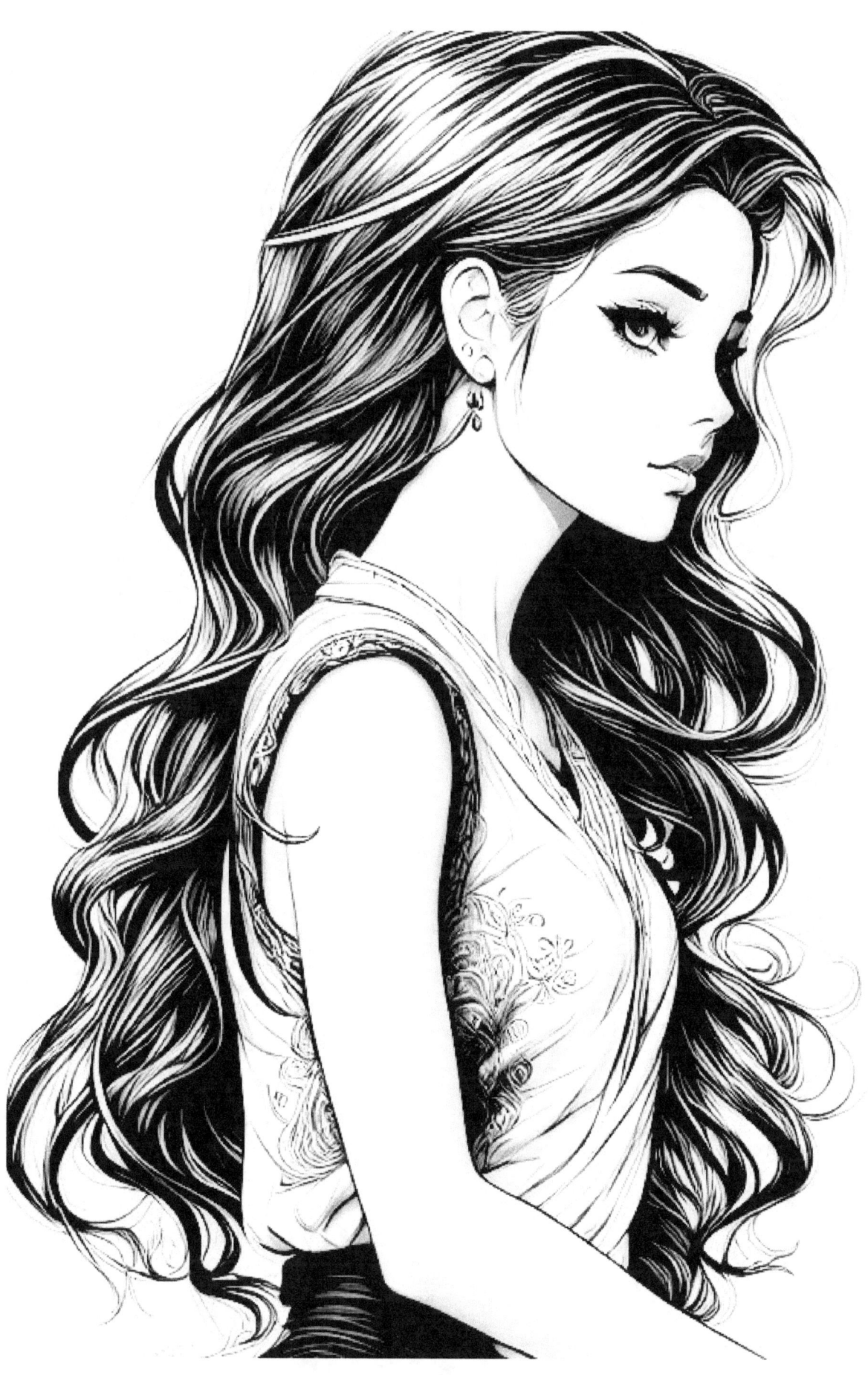

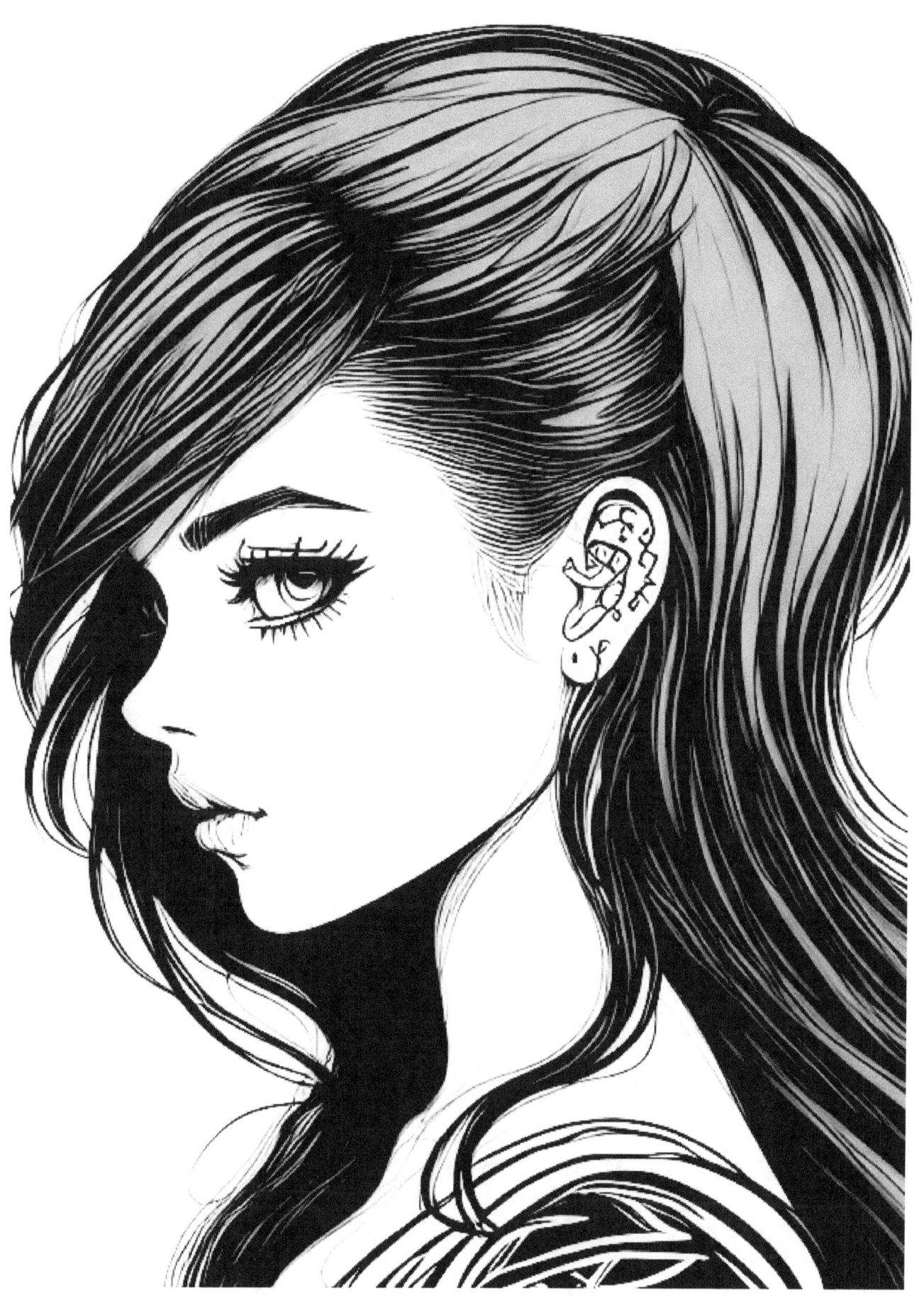

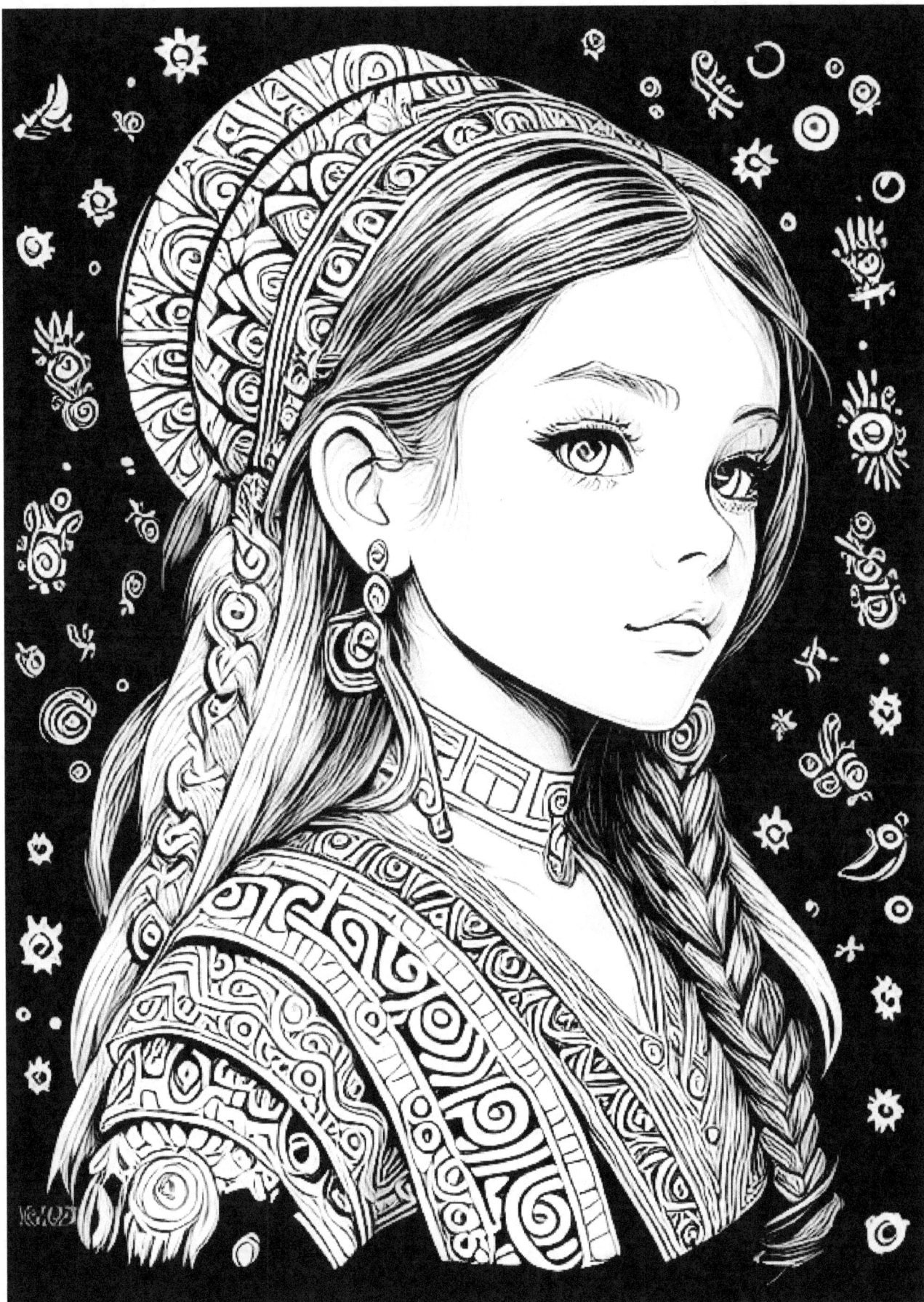

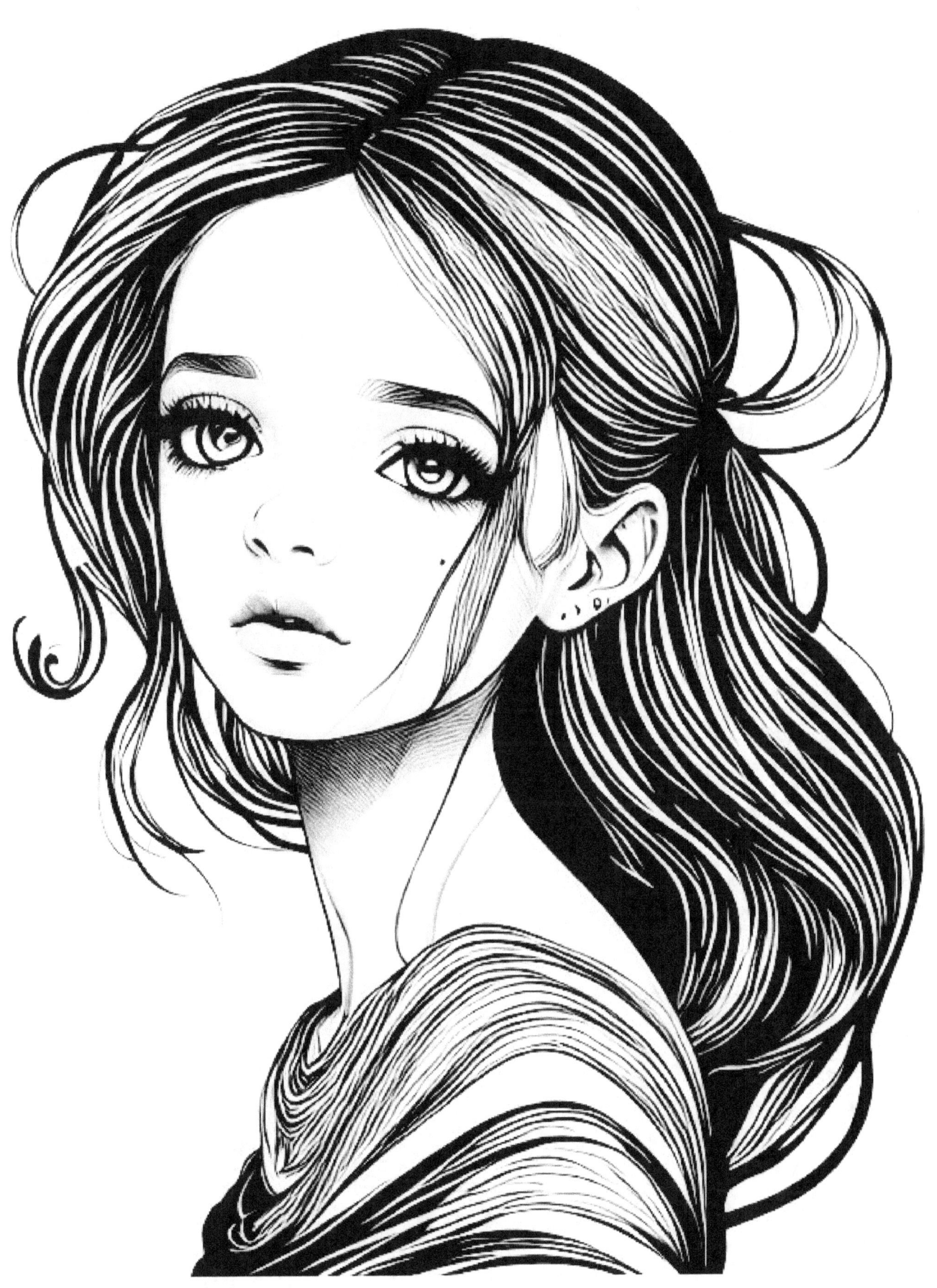

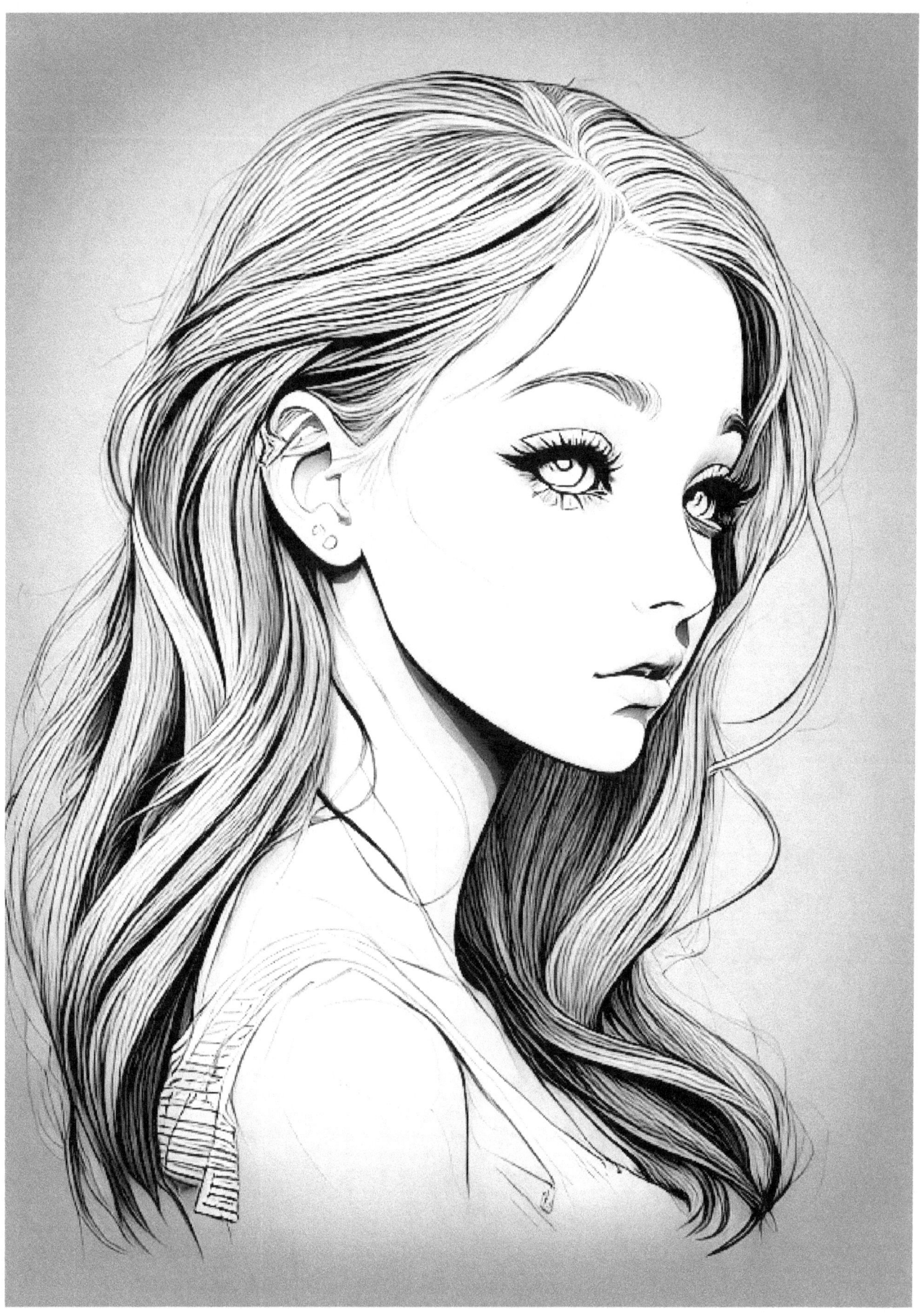

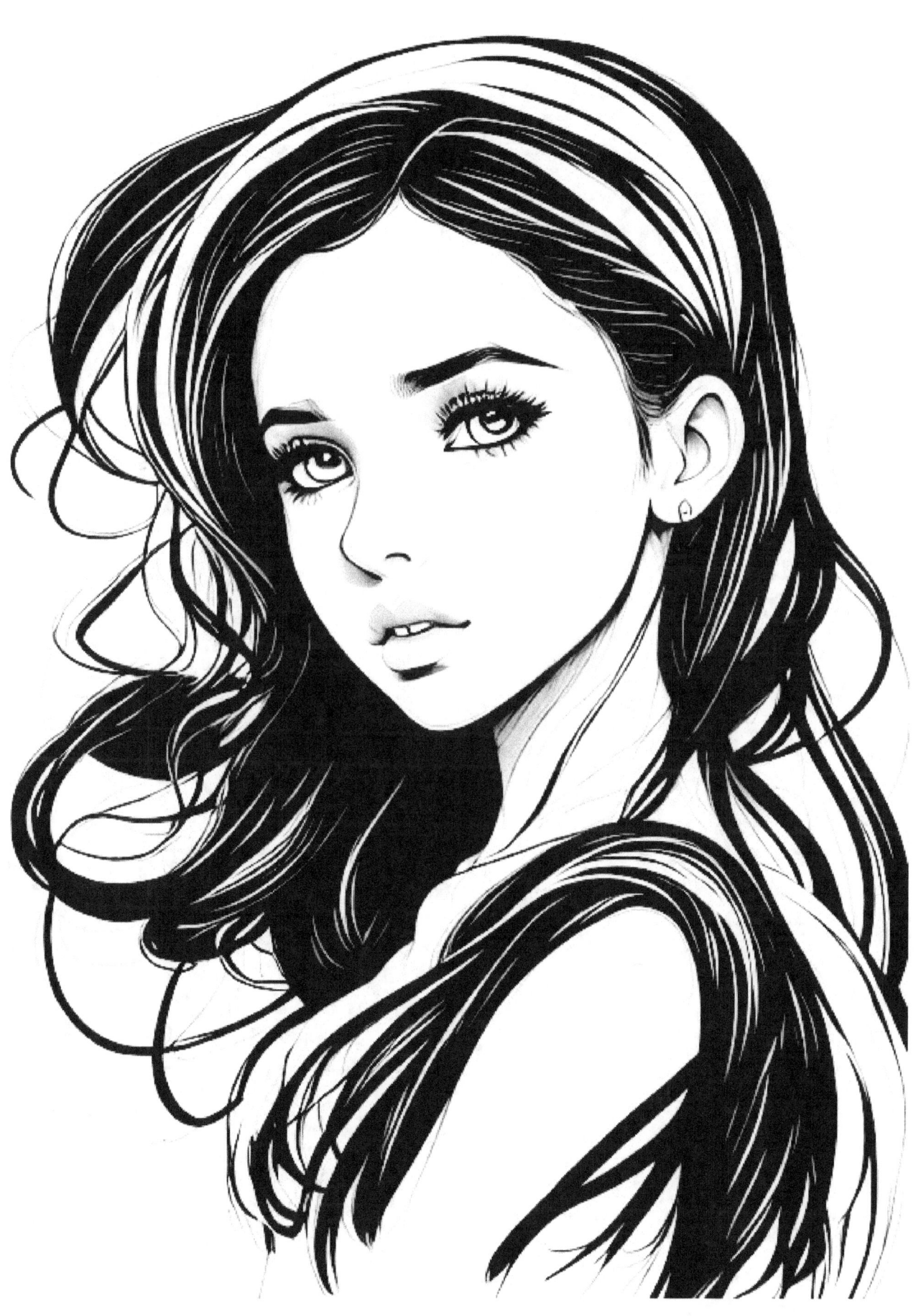

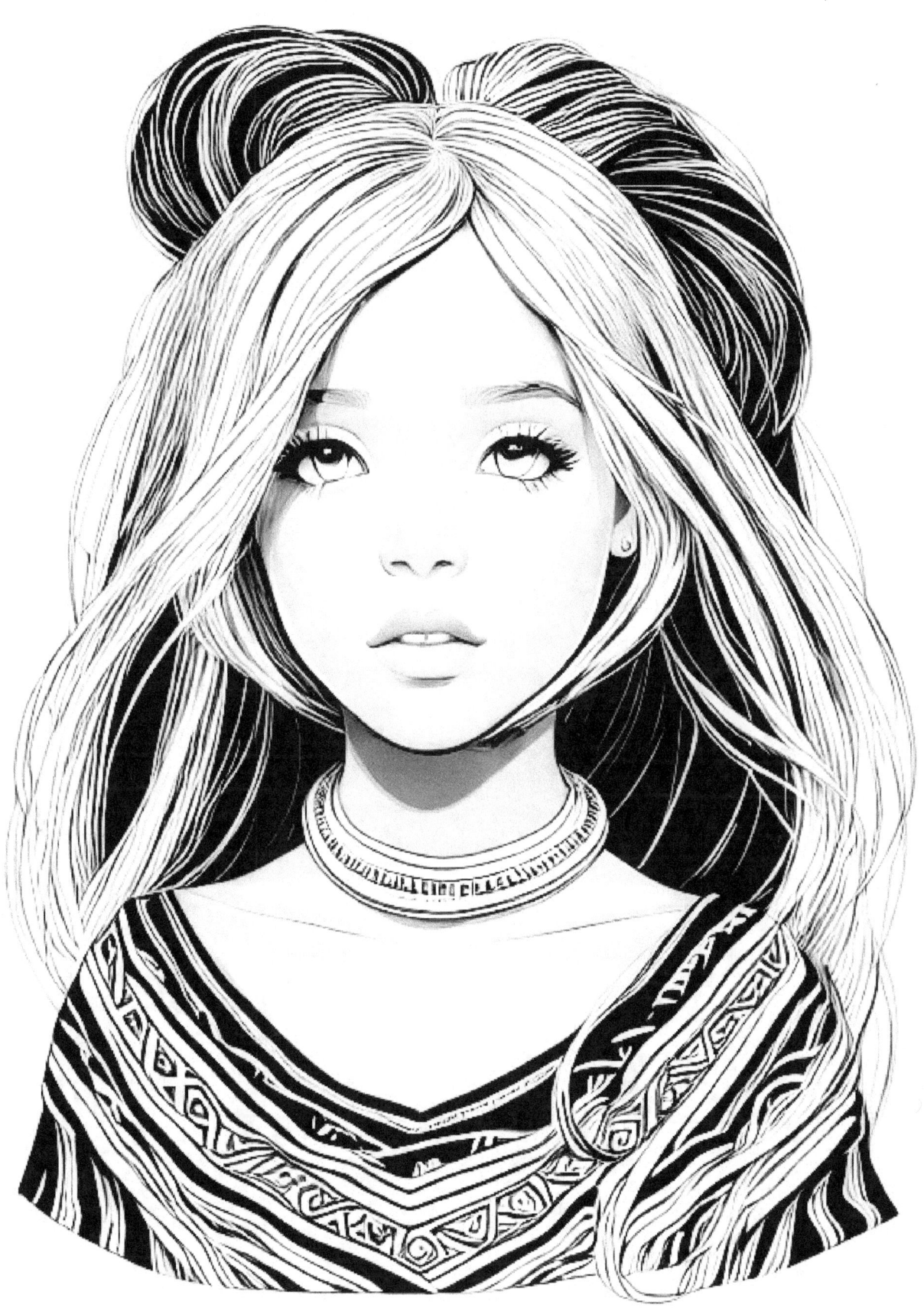

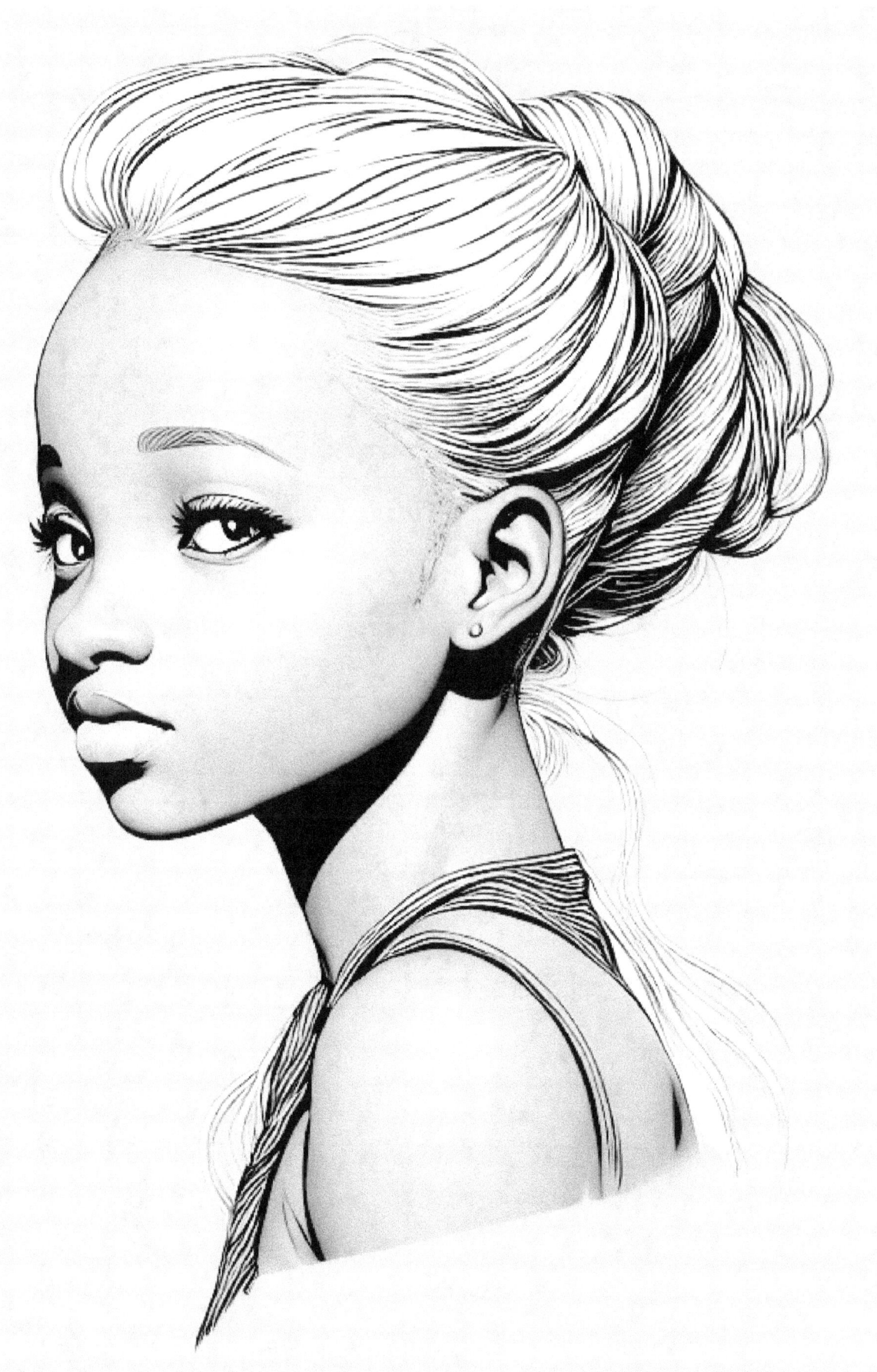

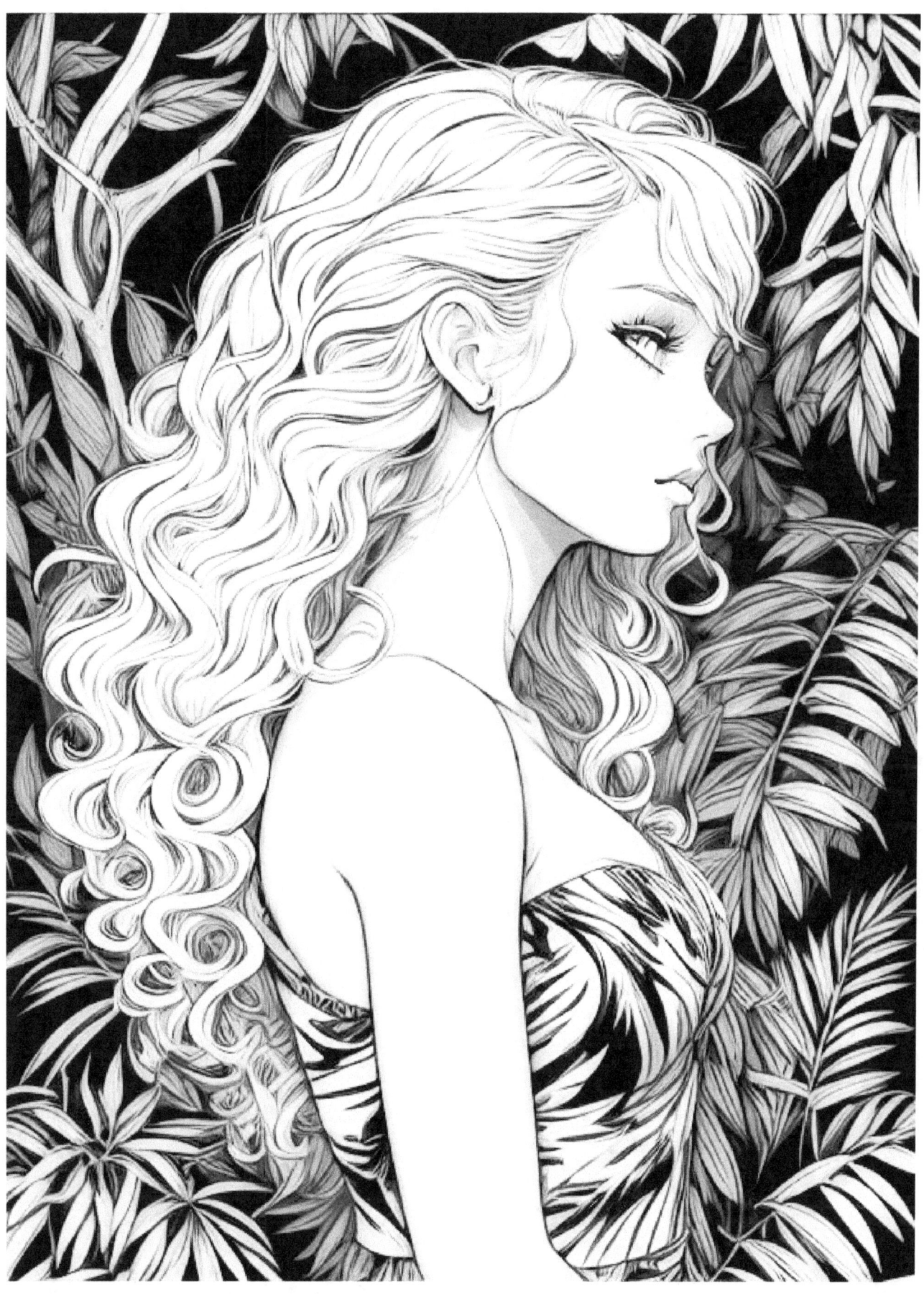

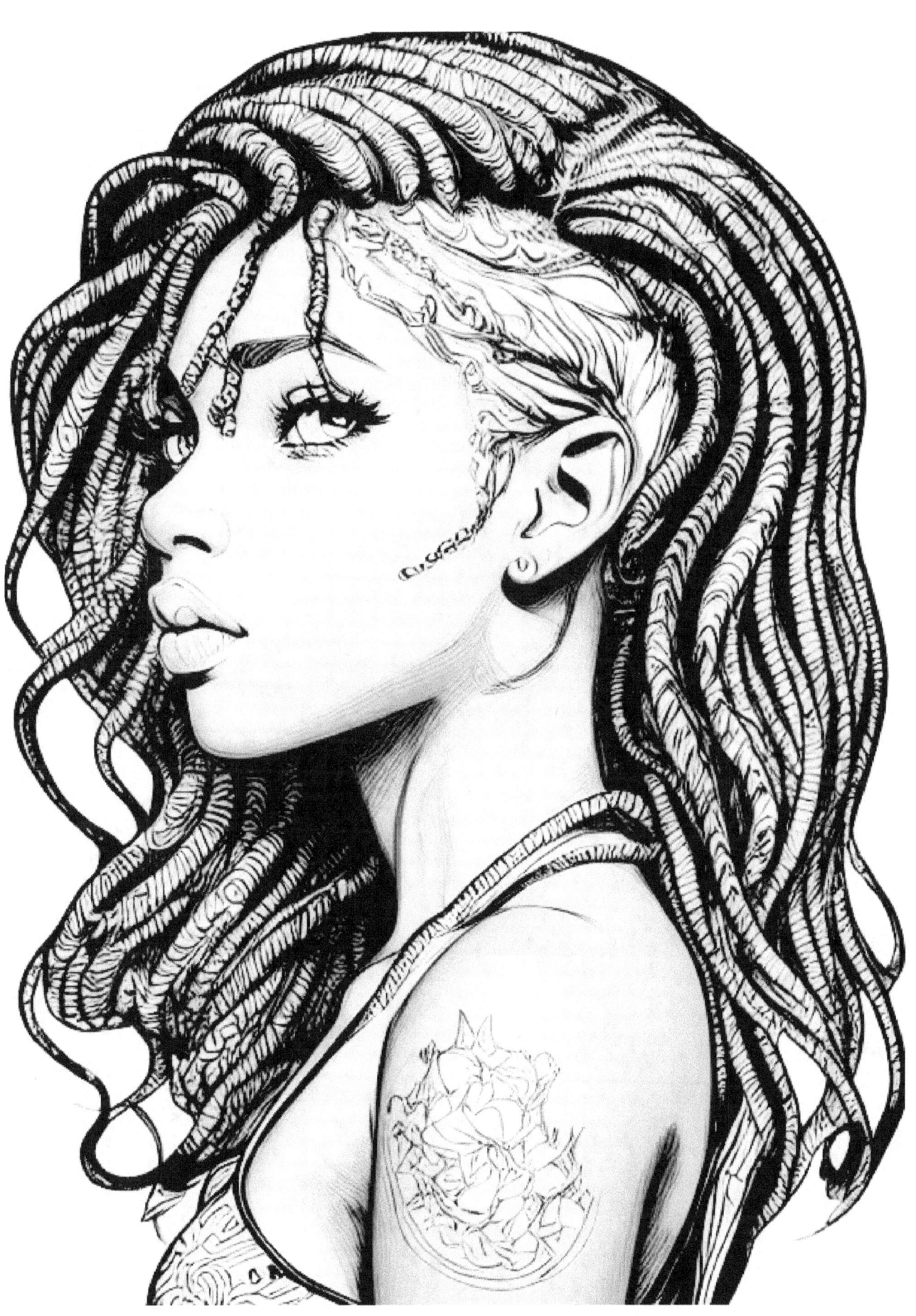

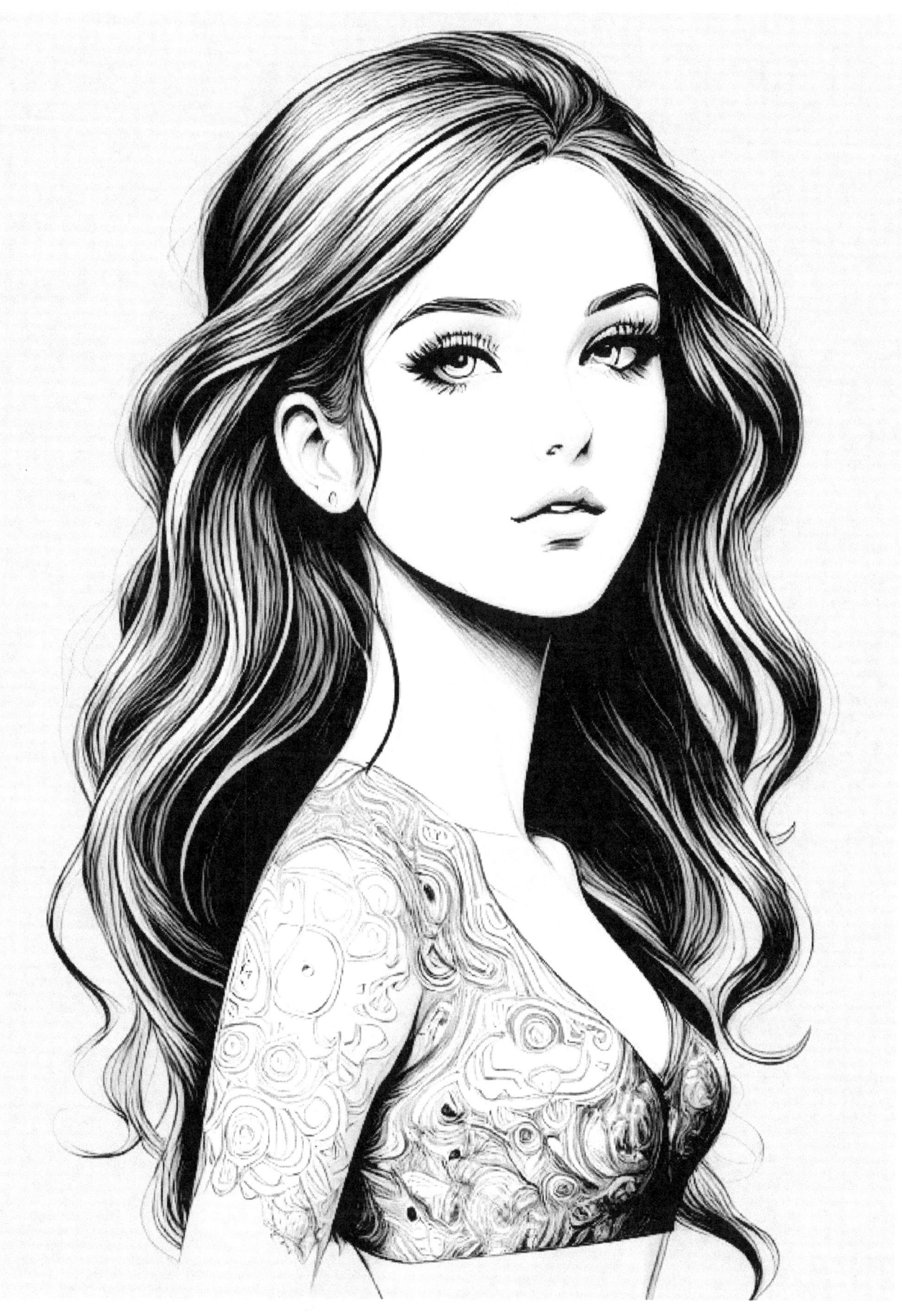

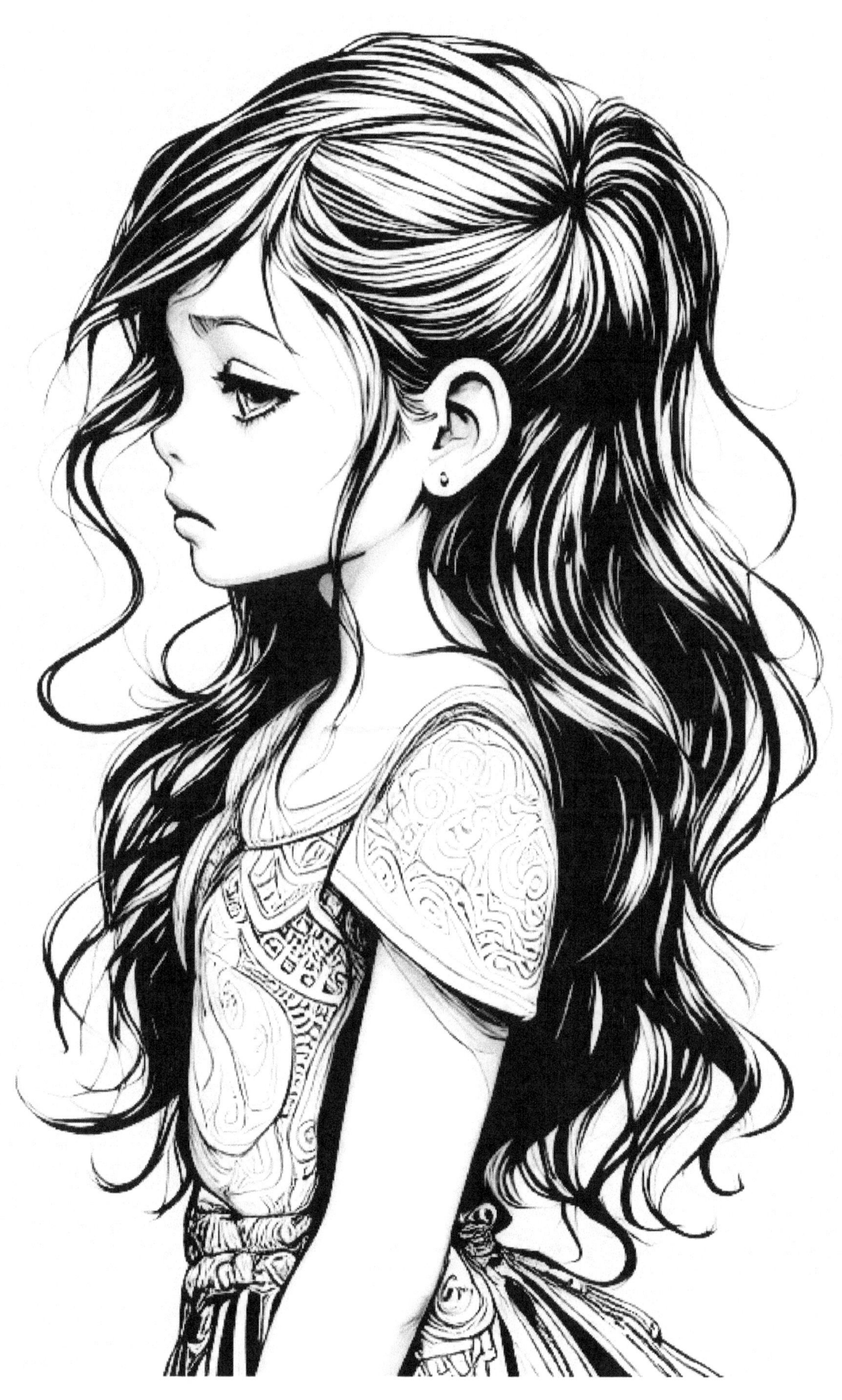

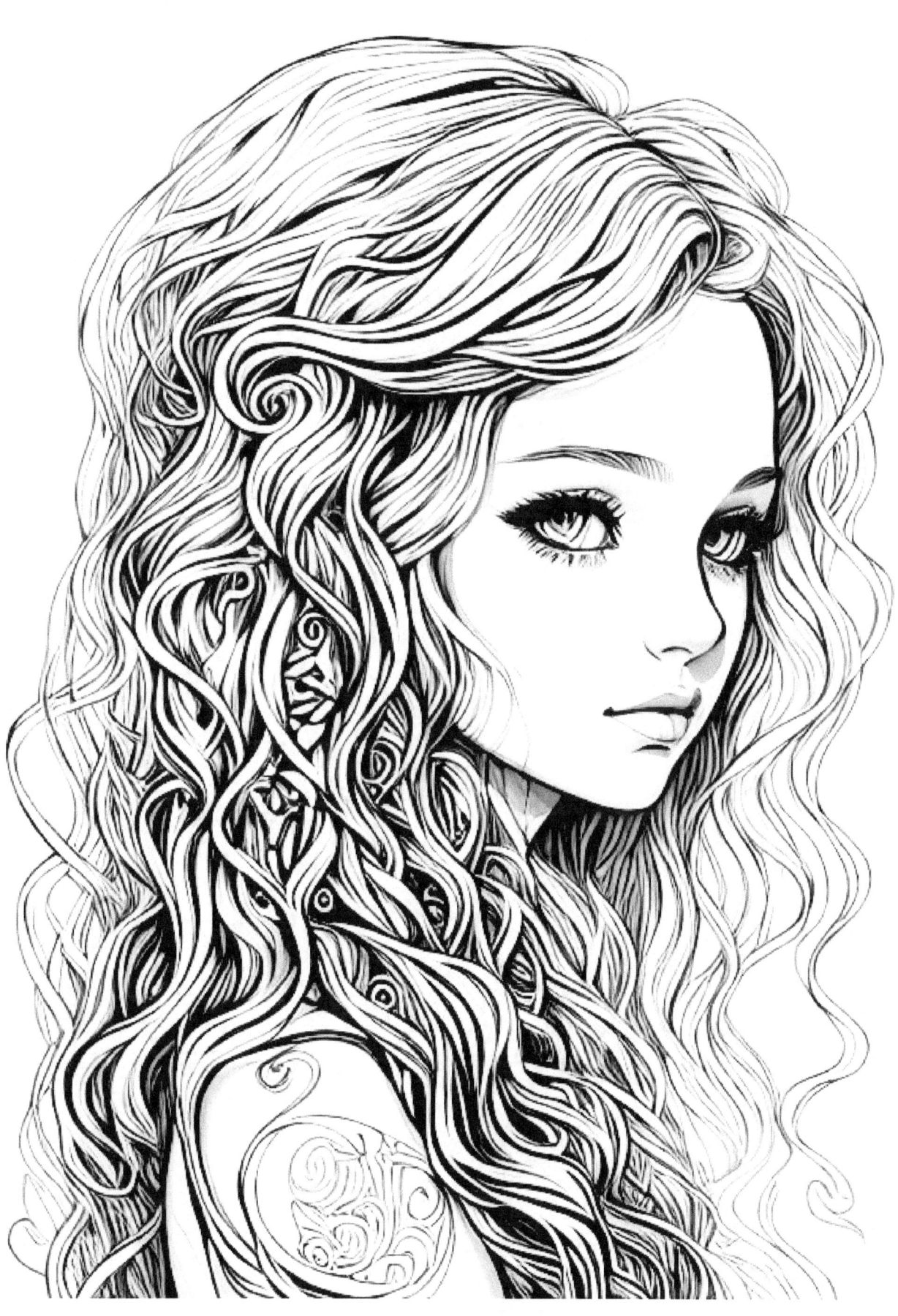

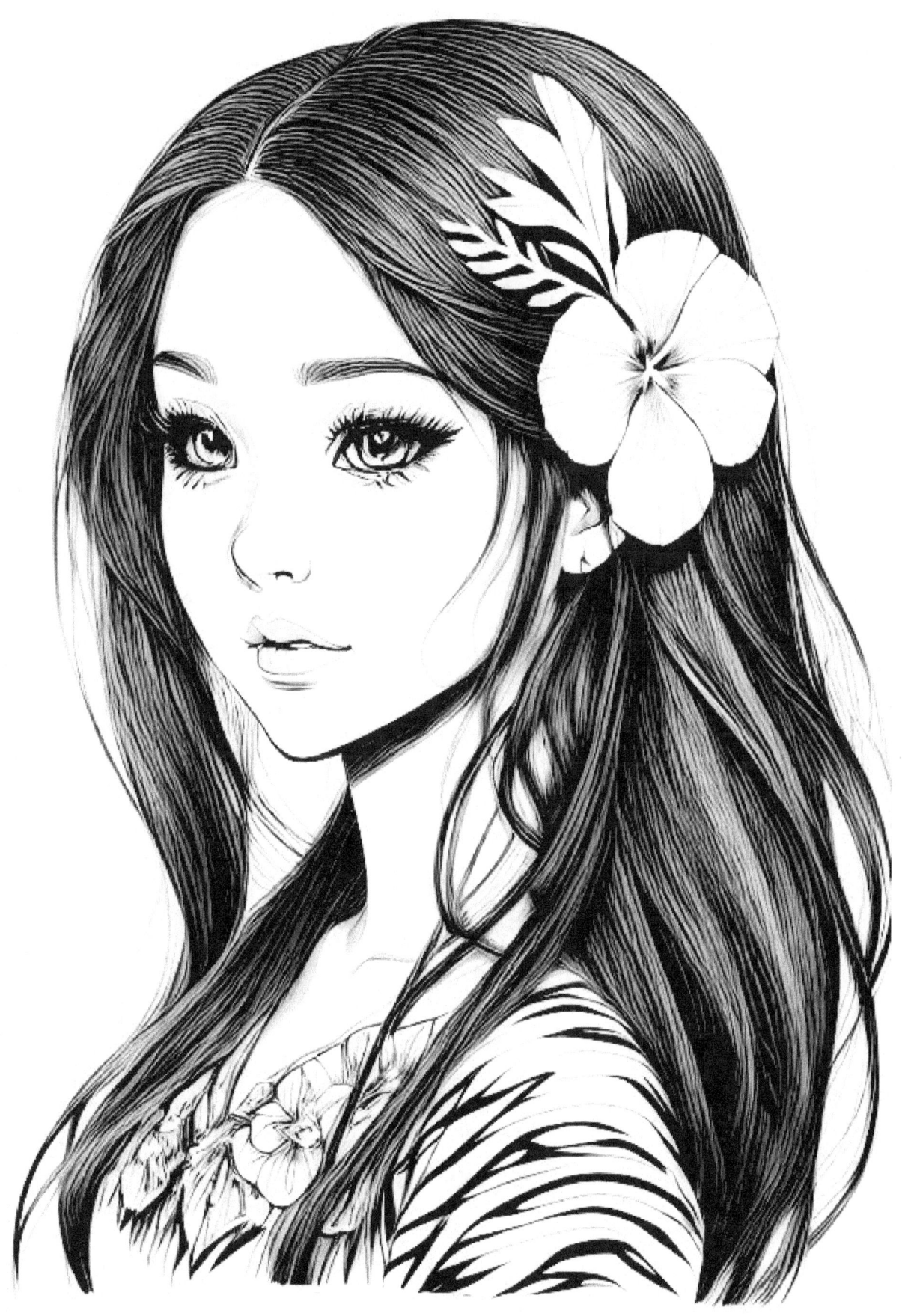

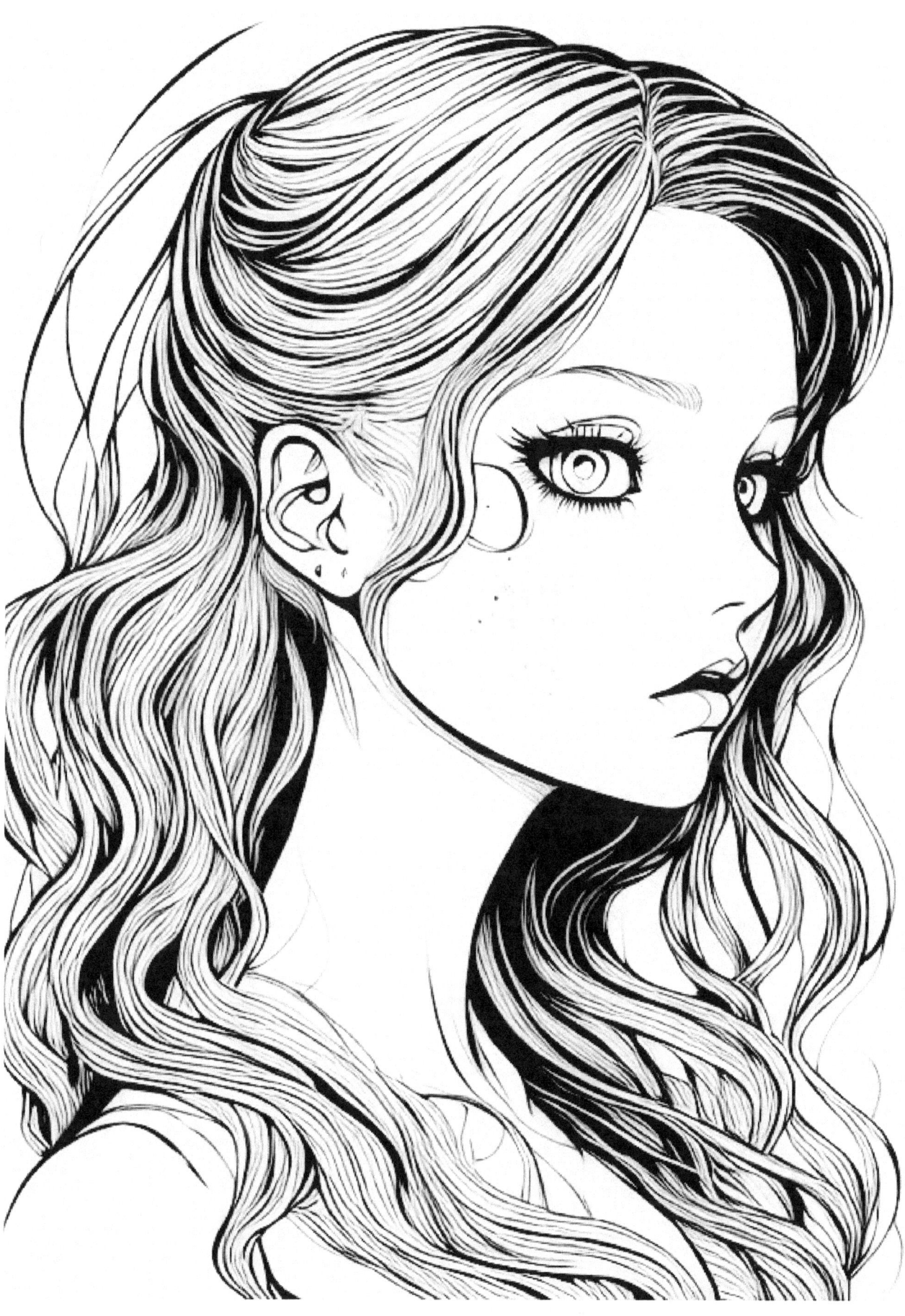

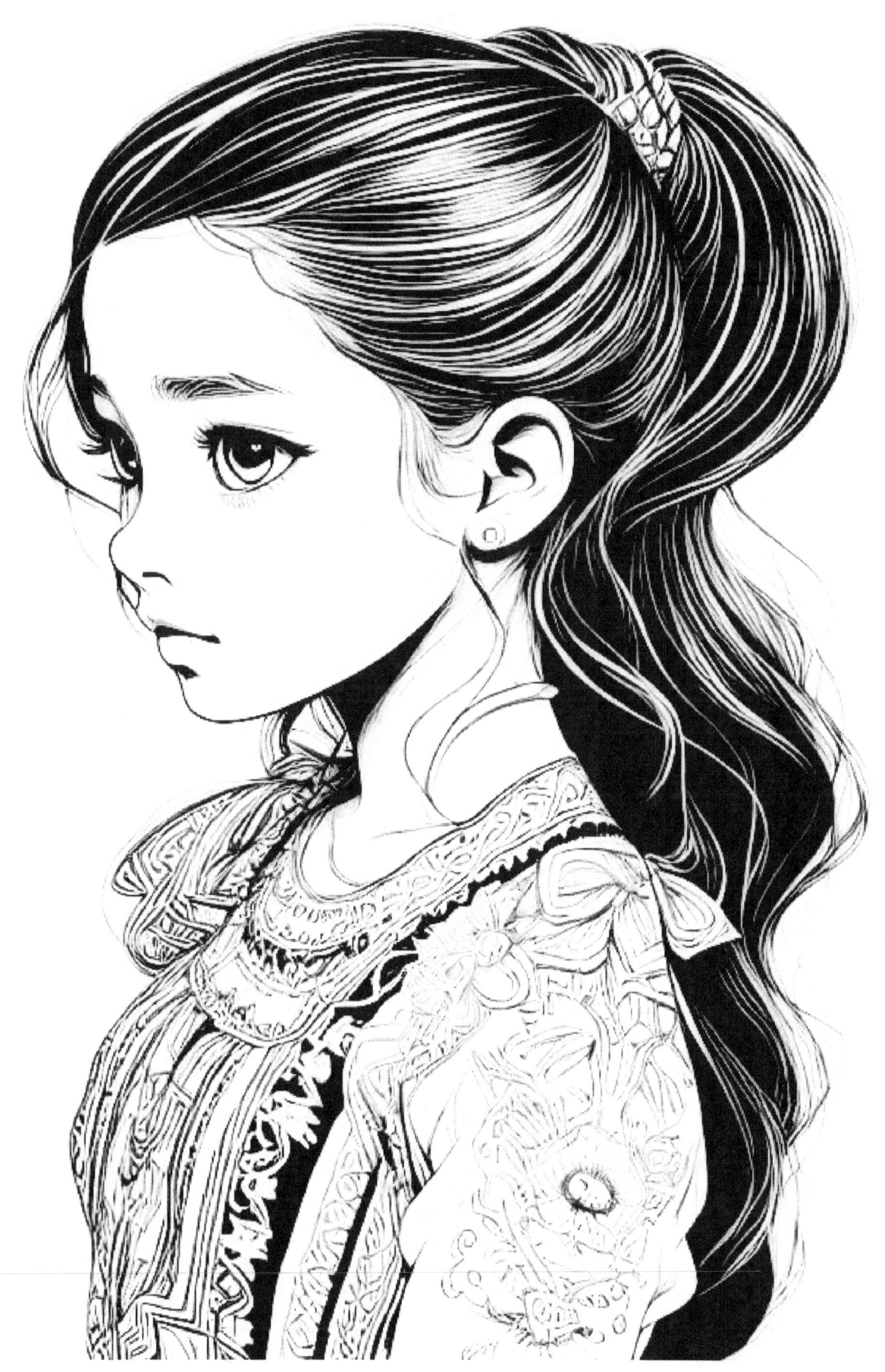

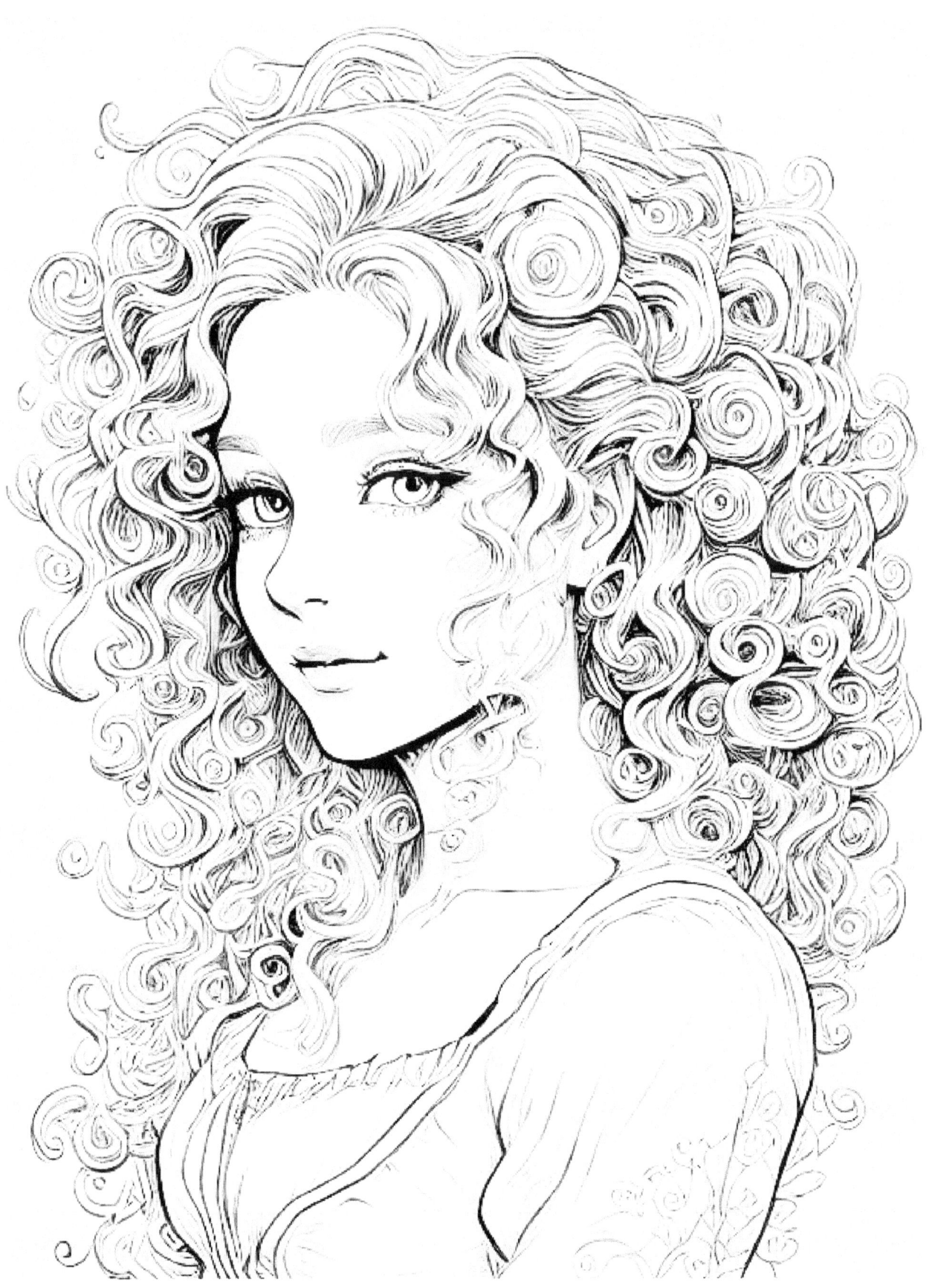

inkventiva

Women of the World
Color Diversity

Let your colors bring out the beauty and uniqueness of these women.

www.ingramcontent.com/pod-product-compliance
Lightning Source LLC
Chambersburg PA
CBHW082147230526

45467CB00043B/2405